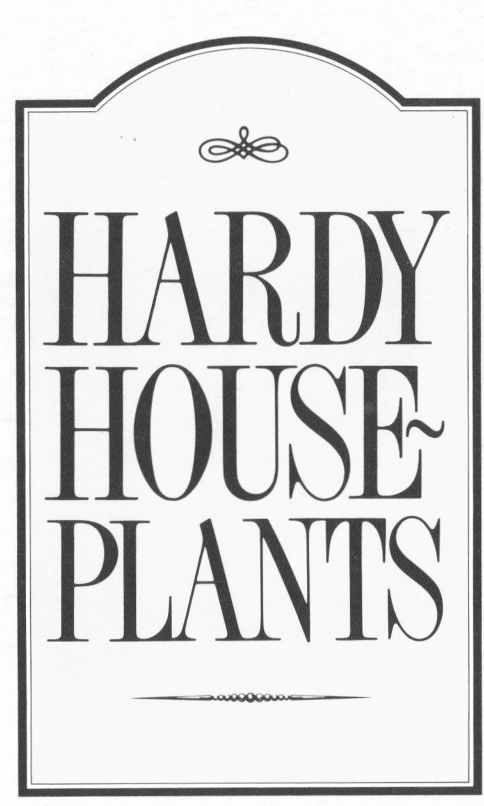
HARDY
HOUSE~
PLANTS

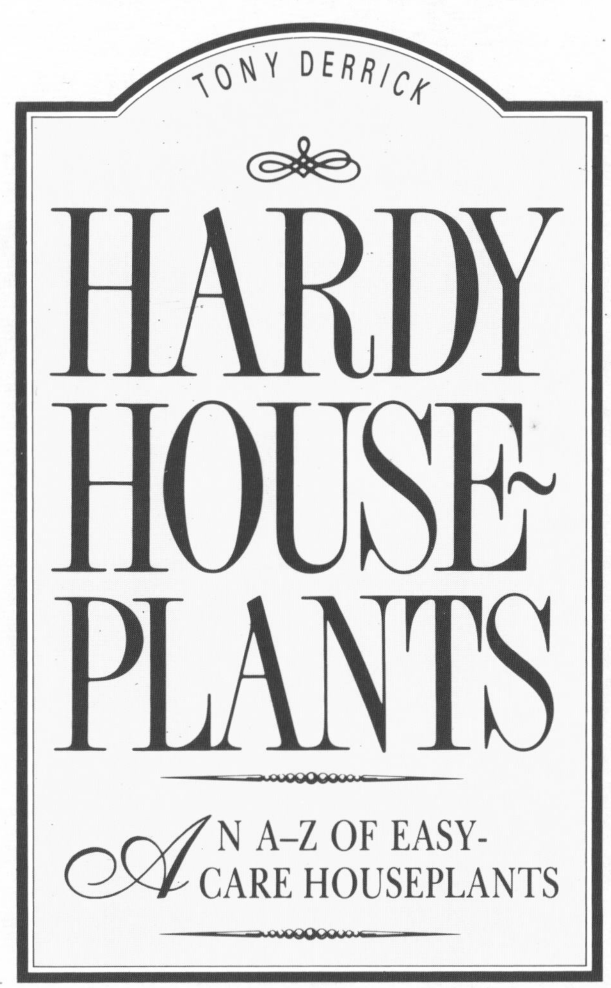
TONY DERRICK
HARDY HOUSE-PLANTS
AN A–Z OF EASY-CARE HOUSEPLANTS

THE APPLE PRESS

A QUINTET BOOK

Published by The Apple Press
6 Blundell Street
London N7 9BH

ISBN 1–85076–126–4

This book was designed and produced by
Quintet Publishing Limited
6 Blundell Street
London N7 9BH

Art Director: Peter Bridgewater
Designer: Annie Moss
Editors: Mike Darton, Shaun Barrington
Photographer: Peter Stiles

Typeset in Great Britain by
Central Southern Typesetters, Eastbourne
Manufactured in Hong Kong by
Regent Publishing Services Limited
Printed in Hong Kong by
South Sea Int'l Press Ltd.

CONTENTS

Introduction

What can surpass the charms of a house-plant gracing a windowsill, in relieving the starkness of a blank wall, or cascading gracefully from a hanging basket? In appreciating such beauty, it is easy to become a collector without realizing it.

The range of plants now offered in florists' shops and garden centres is vast, even bewildering. There are plants of every conceivable size and shape to suit every part of the home. And the plants are not merely good to look at, either. They are *alive*, and bring a special touch of brightness and vitality to the home in a way that no vase or ornament ever could: a breath of the vibrant outdoors, whether the home is a country cottage close to the fields or a city apartment hemmed in by steel, concrete and asphalt.

In fact, plants minister to people's longing for the open countryside — our ancestral habitat. They are forever changing — growing, flowering, resting, ageing, dying. They never allow our interest in them to flag; and they rely upon us for their every need, however modest these may be. In looking after them we build an active relationship with them.

Here, then, are the makings of a fascinating hobby, a hobby that for those who have unlimited spare time could become an obsession. But what if you are busy — as so many of us are in these frantic times?

Such a life-style spells potential disaster for your house-plants. They may perforce be neglected. Yet even one lapse in their regular care can result in brown foliage, withered flowers and fast-multiplying colonies of aphids.

So do you have to forego altogether the pleasures and the company of house-plants? There is actually no real reason to think so. It is the theme of this book to show that by carefully selecting the most resilient, good-tempered kinds of plant which make the minimum of demands, and which recover quickly from the occasional brief period of neglect, it is possible to enjoy many of the benefits of house-plants. As a general rule, however, you will have to deny yourself the keener pleasures of possessing such exotic flowering plants as CINERARIAS, GLOXINIAS or SCHIZANTHUS, which are just too sensitive and temperamental to thrive without frequent and wholehearted attention. (All the same, there is no reason not to indulge yourself with the occasional flowering plant so long as you treat it from the start as temporary and dispensable. Enjoy it for a while, then cast it out without regret.)

For long-term pleasure, however, it is best to look towards resilient foliage plants such as the familiar MONSTERA and FICUS; cheerful, long-suffering trailing TRADESCANTIA and ZEBRINA; and the tough, spiny beauty of the bromeliad group, including the ornamental pineapple itself, AECHMEA and VRIESIA.

Where light is good but space is perhaps at a premium, explore the bizarre fascination of cacti and succulent plants; some have amusing or grotesque shapes, and many have vividly coloured flowers. In shadier spots where little flourishes, look to the fern family, which may be more richly varied than you at first realize.

Be adventurous in your use of plants. Some make impressive specimens in a suitable pot, tub or *jardinière*. But experiment additionally with grouping several plants of contrasting shape, colour and leaf texture in a bowl or an urn. Create a miniature desert garden with cacti and rocks, or train an evergreen climber (such as a PHILODENDRON) up a mossy pole to form a vertical accent in your room.

Plants benefit from each other's company, their beauty accentuated by contrast with that of their neighbours, their wellbeing improved by the more congenial growing conditions in a larger container. Grouping plants is dealt with at greater length on pp.00-00.

It is essential to remember, however, that even the least demanding of house-plants needs some regular care and responds favourably to something more than the minimum of attention. One of our most important considerations, therefore, is how we may keep our plants thriving, skilfully yet economically.

Light, Air and Temperature

Plants are often used as if they were ornaments about the house. But never be tempted to think of them merely as objects to be admired — occasionally dusted or freshened up, but otherwise ignored. This is undoubtedly a recipe for disaster. It is vital to remember that every plant is a living thing: it has needs that must be satisfied if it is to survive. And in the artificial environment of your home it relies entirely upon you to supply those needs.

It is helpful to think of a plant as a chemical factory powered by sunlight. All its processes interact; if it lacks any basic ingredient or the light or warmth to power those processes, therefore, it plainly cannot flourish. To function, it needs light and air, warmth, water, food, and usually an annual rest period. Some climbers, for instance, also need some physical support. All these factors are so closely interdependent that none can be said to be more important than another. All need to be balanced in order to provide a stable environment. If the temperature rises, for example, more water and ventilation are needed to keep the plant comfortable; 75°F (24°C) is the common upper limit.

Actually, it is remarkable that we can grow such a varied range of plants in our homes (and something to be very thankful for). Not only are plants' needs varied, but our homes are designed and managed for *our* comfort, not for that of our plants. Their preferences in fact often conflict with ours — notably in the matter of humidity. Few of us could relax in the permanently humid atmosphere of a warm greenhouse. Equally, our plants are less likely to flourish in a dry atmosphere in which they also become more vulnerable to insect attack – notably by red spider mite.

Foliage plants such as MONSTERA and the PHILODENDRONS from the tropical forests enjoy a daily drenching over their foliage, but it is difficult to provide that in a beautifully furnished lounge. Compromise by misting their foliage from a hand sprayer, and take them outdoors occasionally for a more generous wetting.

Light can also be a problem. Windowsill plants tend to receive light from only one side, so their growth becomes lopsided unless they are turned regularly to give each side full light in its turn. Away from the windows, and particularly in dimly lit hallways, light is inadequate for many plants — cacti, for example, fail to thrive. For such locations we should rather utilize shade-loving ferns or evergreen foliage plants adapted for growth beneath the dense canopy of giant rain-forest trees in the tropics.

To be sensitive to our plants' needs and to supply them when and to the degree required may seem a most formidable proposition if spare time is limited. In practice, however, some needs are adequately catered for by careful siting; some fortunately require only occasional attention; and others in any event quickly become part of the domestic routine. It is easy soon to enjoy caring for your plants.

LIGHT

Most plants seem to smile in the sunshine — unless of course they are shade-loving ferns. They develop a healthier glow and open their flowers more freely. But the main reason for giving plants all the light they can get is that it provides the energy for their chemical processes, and thus facilitates their growth.

All plants contain green chlorophyll which traps the energy from sunlight, even when it is dim. By the process known as photosynthesis, the chlorophyll then utilizes the light to manufacture sugars and other complex chemicals from the hydrogen and oxygen in water, from carbon in the carbon dioxide absorbed from the air, and from minerals derived from the soil in which they are growing.

AIR AND VENTILATION

Most of us like to get some fresh air into our homes when we can, and house-plants appreciate fresh air too. But whereas we are seeking a fresh influx of oxygen, the plants are more in need of carbon dioxide to help in their food manufacture. Humans and plants both welcome the effect of ventilation, provided that it is warm enough, that it clears any fumes from fires or cooking, and that it does not result in draughts or gusts of cold air. For plants, moving air also discourages fungus diseases, because the fungal spores cannot settle and germinate.

Always ventilate with some thought to the outdoor conditions, however, and never to excess. And be ready to give your plants more water to compensate for the moisture removed by the air currents.

TEMPERATURE

Because so many foliage plants come from the tropical forests, and because most cacti are desert plants, you might well think that the hotter you keep your house, the more the house-plants will like it. But this is not so. Provided that you can ensure temperatures between 45°F (7°C) and 75°F (24°C) — a range most people maintain for their own comfort in any case — you need have few worries about your plants' susceptibilities. A far more likely problem is that of humidity (which is discussed later).

Never think of house-plants as 'hot-house' plants. Many do enjoy high temperatures, but the warmth must be accompanied by suitable humidity and good light. Unless you can provide these in the degree normal for a botanic garden glasshouse, it is better to aim for a good balance between them at a more modest 65-70°F (18-21°C).

It is even more important to avoid widely fluctuating temperatures, which few plants can cope with happily. Centrally-heated rooms in which the heat goes off at night, or window sills that are roasted by direct sunlight are but two examples of conditions to avoid.

Watering and Feeding

WATERING

'How much water should I give my plants?' is the most frequent of all questions about house-plant care. Give them too little and their leaves droop and shrivel, perhaps beyond recovery; too much and the foliage yellows and the roots rot. So how is it possible to strike a comfortable balance between these extremes?

Above all, think in terms of each plant's needs of the moment — which vary according to the species of plant, its maturity, the time of year, and the temperature. Don't expect to give it a fixed amount of water at fixed intervals. Learn to recognize when it needs water. Fill its pot to the rim, then leave it alone until it is dry again and ready for another drink.

The best guide to how thirsty a plant is is the state of the surface compost. If the top ½ in (1.3 cm) is dry, the plant needs watering.

How often do plants need watering? It varies, generally from three times a week in summer to once a week (or even less often) in winter. But it is advisable to develop your own watering regime first by frequently inspecting your plants, and then by watering when they require it. By selecting the more resilient kinds of house-plant (as we have here), you may be able to reduce your summer care to a twice-weekly inspection and watering. The need for water can be reduced, and your plants kept healthier, if their surroundings are also kept more humid (as discussed below).

Most house-plants respond well to this kind of watering regime — but there are exceptions. The sedge CYPERUS ALTERNIFOLIUS is one of the few that likes to be wet all the time. Cacti and succulents, on the other hand, watered like other plants when dry in spring and summer, should be kept almost dry in winter — provided that they are not allowed to shrivel — or they may well start rotting.

ABOVE The leaves of this Ficus pumila *are dehydrated.*

RIGHT This croton has wilted disastrously because of root loss caused by over-watering.

*ABOVE The Bird's Nest Fern (*Asplenium nidus*) is a superb foliage plant (page 33). It contrasts well with the orange-flowered Goldfish Plant. Both enjoy the humidity of the bathroom.*

Bromeliads are a further distinct group. Be sure to keep the funnel or vase formed by their leaves topped up with water. The very open, fibrous, well-drained compost in which they stand can be kept just moist.

Always water thoroughly and leave alone for a time afterward. Do not give frequent dribbles of water, or the surface soil will become wet while the rest of the soil ball remains dry as dust, or the plants themselves may become waterlogged. Neither of these scenarios encourages plant growth.

HUMIDITY

The air in our homes, particularly in winter when the central heating is operating, tends to be much drier than plants like. Tropical plants revel in warmth, but in their native areas it is accompanied by frequent downpours of rain and high humidity.

Although we cannot damp down our rooms as is done in a botanic garden glasshouse, we can still improve humidity for our plants by standing them on trays or saucers of pebbles which are kept moist, so humidifying the air around their leaves. Grouping plants in larger containers packed with damp peat also improves local humidity. Misting with water from a hand sprayer is an additional way to imitate the freshness of a tropical downpour.

REST PERIOD

Some plants have an obvious dormant period each year. Bulbs such as the hippeastrums, for instance, lose their leaves, then begin another cycle of growth after a rest. During a rest period, reduce watering to a minimum and cease feeding altogether. Although the popular foliage plants do not become dormant, they do become far less active in winter, so again stop feeding and reduce watering . Forcing growth at this time only harms plants.

HOLIDAYS

Leaving the home empty for any continuous period requires the conscientious plant owner to come to an arrangement with a helpful neighbour to water the plants, or failing that, to provide some temporary form of automatic watering. Stand plants on capillary matting in a sink, kept moist by a dripping tap, or in a bath with an inch (1.3 cm) of water in the bottom. Even wrapping a recently watered plant in a large plastic bag secured with a tag can be sufficient to keep it going while you are away.

ABOVE *The marvellous trumpet-shaped flower of the hippeastrum; hippeastrums are one of the bulb flowers which are not difficult to grow indoors.*

POTTING, SOIL MIXTURES, FEEDING

House-plants you buy will already be growing in a suitable medium — a peat-based or soil-based mixture containing enough fertilizer to keep the plants fed for a couple of months. After that they will need regular feeding during the active season of growth. Although powdered fertilizer can be dusted on to the soil surface and water in, or fertilizer tablets or sticks thrust into the compost, a dilute liquid fertilizer is simpler to use and easier to regulate according to the plants' needs. Administer weak doses at frequent intervals rather than occasional large ones.

Plants that are growing well in 3- or 4-in (7½- or 10-cm) pots soon fill the pots with roots and require larger pots with greater reserves of compost, food and moisture. Inspect each plant's roots by supporting the surface of the rootball on your left hand and tapping the rim of the pot on a bench until the rootball drops out. If it is massed with white roots, it is time to move the plant into a larger pot.

Select one about 1 in (2.5 cm) larger in diameter; arrange some broken pieces of clay flowerpot over the drainage hole; then spread enough potting mixture over this to raise the surface of the plant's rootball to ½ in (1.3 cm) below the rim of the new pot. Set the plant in place; then fill round with more compost, firming moderately as you go. Finally, tap the pot on a hard surface to settle the compost, and water in carefully.

Plants which are already in larger pots, and which cannot easily be repotted, can be given a fresh lease of life by top dressing instead. Remove 1-2 in (2.5-5 cm) of exhausted compost from the surface of the rootball in spring (when growth starts in earnest) and replace with fresh.

Never move a plant into a pot that is larger than necessary. Compost that is not being explored by plant roots soon becomes stagnant with frequent watering, and stagnation discourages root growth.

Peat-based composts are excellent but are dependent upon regular feeding. They are also difficult to rewet if they dry out. Soil-based composts contain more plant foods but still need feeding, and often tend to compact with watering, becoming hard and airless, depressing plant growth. An equal-parts mix of the two kinds suits many.

Tall, leafy plants in plastic pots can become top-heavy and fall over unless stones are placed in the bottom of the pot or heavy, coarse sand is added to the mixture.

DRAINAGE

Plants' roots need oxygen as well as food and water in order to grow healthily, so the soil mixture in which they grow must be well drained and of an open, porous texture that holds air, even after a thorough watering. If it does not, the soil becomes stagnant and the roots could rot.

Plant Problems

Well tended plants provided with suitable light, warmth, moisture and food seldom suffer from the various problems — physical, insect or disease — that can afflict them. But a conscientious grower must be able to recognize them if they should arise in order to deal with them promptly.

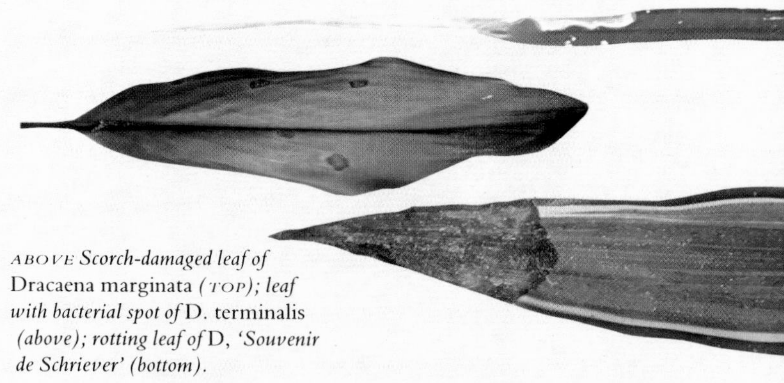

ABOVE Scorch-damaged leaf of Dracaena marginata *(TOP); leaf with bacterial spot of* D. terminalis *(above); rotting leaf of* D. *'Souvenir de Schriever' (bottom).*

PHYSICAL

Falling or unhealthy leaves — a sure sign that something is wrong with a plant — are a frequent cause of anxiety. But if you interpret your plant's signal correctly, and adjust your care for it accordingly, the problem should soon be overcome.

It is quite normal for an occasional lower leaf to turn yellow and fall — from a FICUS ELASTICA, for example. But if many leaves do so you are overwatering your plant or it is objecting to a cold draught. Brown, drying lower leaves, on the other hand, are a sign of underwatering, poor light or excessive warmth.

A sudden leaf fall follows a shock to the plant — a sharp fluctuation in temperatures, perhaps, or drought at the roots. Wilting (drooping) leaves show that the plant is too hot, located in too bright sunlight, short of water, or being overwatered. A quick look at the soil should indicate which of these problems it is. Leaves that curl and later fall are a sign of low temperatures, cold draughts or overwatering.

The development of brown tips or margins on green leaves can have a variety of causes — dry air, over- or under-watering, too much sun, physical bruising, overfeeding, excessive warmth, or not enough of it. These may seem contradictory, but by considering all the other symptoms you should be able to discern which is the cause.

If growth at the top of the plant is pale and spindly, it is suffering from poor light, or from too much warmth, overfeeding and watering during the poorly lit conditions of winter. Remove this weak growth and so encourage the plant to form healthier growth.

Bleached leaves either have received too strong a dose of sunshine or are under attack from red spider mites, sucking out the sap.

BELOW, LEFT TO RIGHT split leaf of Aspidistra elatior, *caused by overfeeding; scorch mark from a radiator on same plant; withered leaf of* Cissus antarctica, *the result of overwatering; brown marks on an otherwise healthy Cissus caused by a sudden chill, or too much light.*

Yellow leaves at the top of the plant indicate an iron or magnesium deficiency because limy water has been given to a lime-hating plant. Use rainwater instead.

Black, rotting leaves are a sure sign of overwatering or poorly drained soil.

Holes in leaves may have been caused by earwigs or caterpillars — or just by careless people or pets.

Why do flowering plants not bloom? They may not be sufficiently mature, but the problem is more likely to be the result of poor light, dry air, too short or too long a period of light each day, or overfeeding, which promotes foliage at the expense of flowers.

Flowers fade quickly if the air or soil is too dry, the temperature too high or the light poor. Flower buds fall in similar conditions of inadequate moisture, poor light, or the shock of fluctuating water or light supply.

MOST COMMON PESTS

APHIDS (GREENFLY): Colonies of green, grey, orange or black insects that suck sap from the soft parts of plants, notably shoot tips and flower buds. They also congregate on the backs of leaves. Their feeding weakens plants, and they leave a sticky deposit of honeydew which predisposes toward black sooty mould (see below). Spray promptly with derris, malathion, or a systemic insecticide.

EARWIG: Not often found on house-plants, but they love to chew the petals and young leaves of chrysanthemums, leaving ragged holes. They are active at night. Search the foliage and pick off the insects by hand.

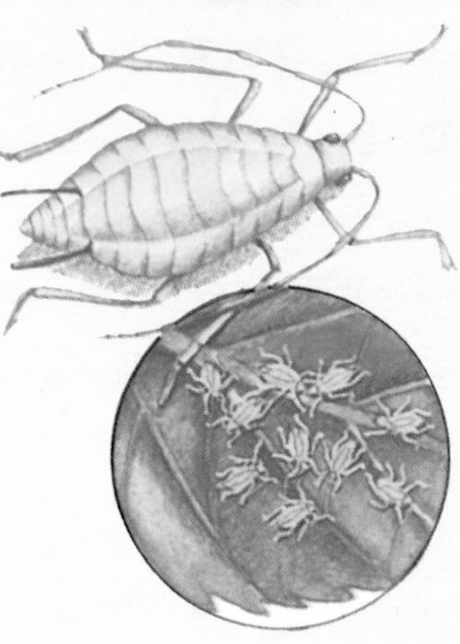

ABOVE Aphid infestation weakens and distorts the plant.

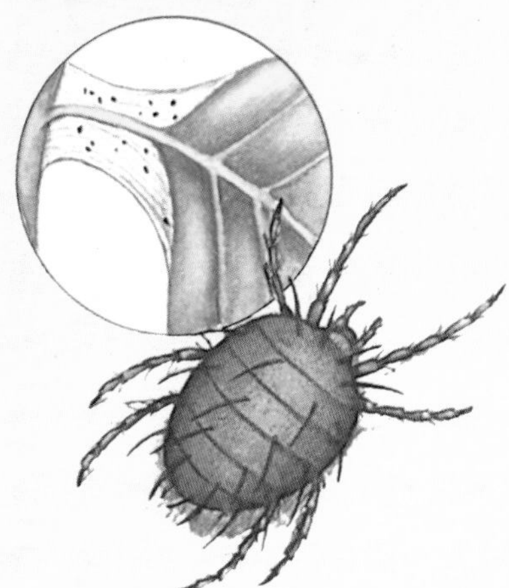

ABOVE Red spider mite infestation on Chamaedorea elegans.

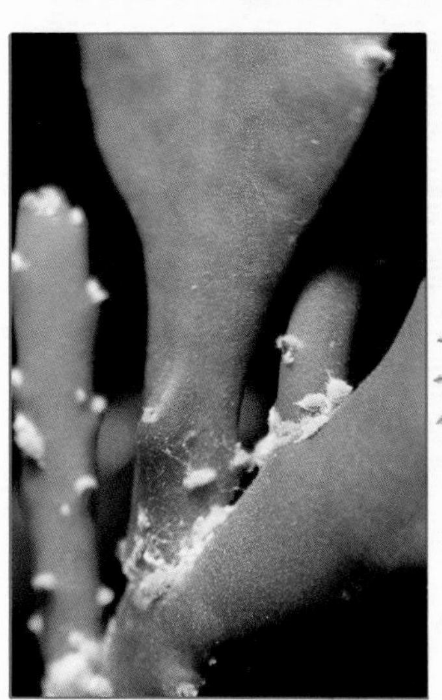

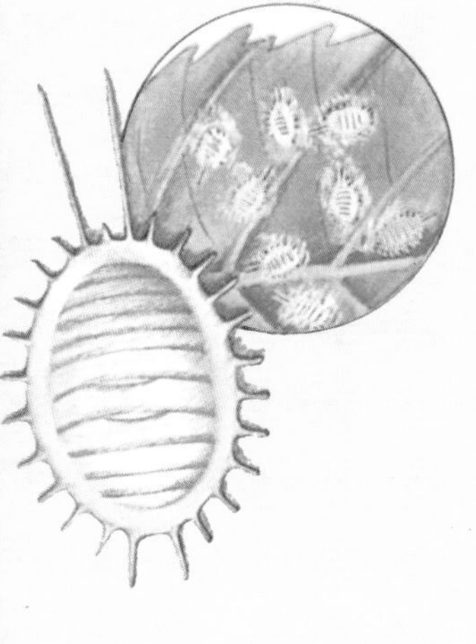

ABOVE AND LEFT Mealy bugs are fairly easy to spot.

MEALY BUG: Small bugs enclosed in a cottony white fluff, which can form large colonies on stems and in leaf joints on many plants, including cacti. Wipe off or dab small colonies with a cloth dipped in methylated spirit (methyl alcohol). Spray with malathion or a systemic insecticide if necessary.

RED SPIDER MITE: Minute sap-sucking insect which can quickly infest plants in a hot, dry atmosphere. Leaves show white or yellow speckling, sometimes small spiders' webs. Keep foliage moist by misting. Spray with systemic insecticide, derris or malathion as soon as noticed.

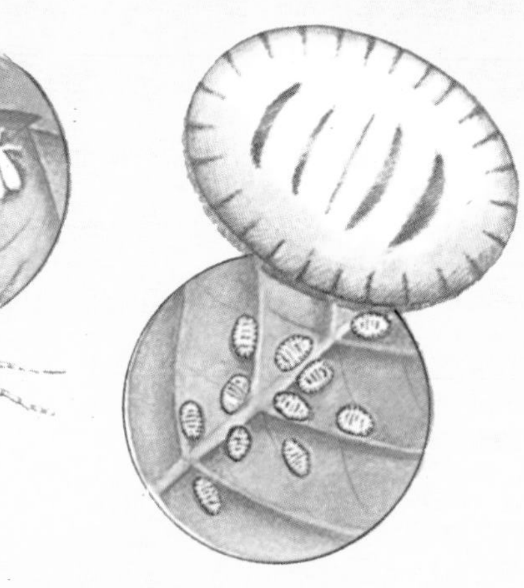

ABOVE Whitefly are difficult to eradicate quickly.

ABOVE The brown scale insect is obvious when attached to green foliage.

SCALE INSECT: Small stationary brown discs attached to stems or against midribs beneath leaves, where they suck sap and exude honeydew, weakening the plant. Remove with a damp cloth before they can multiply. Use systemic insecticide.

WHITEFLY: Tiny white-winged insects that rise in a cloud if disturbed. They multiply rapidly, their larvae suck sap, excrete honeydew and debilitate plants. They are difficult to control. Use, systemic insecticide, or a pirimiphos-methyl-based insecticide at four-day intervals until the pests are cleared.

DISEASES

BLACKLEG: Fungus infection that affects stem cuttings, particularly those of pelargonium. It usually occurs where compost is overwatered, poorly drained and not well aerated. Remove and burn infected cuttings. Provide more suitable conditions in future.

GREY MOULD (BOTRYTIS): Grey fluffy fungus growth that attacks the soft parts of plants, or damaged tissue, particularly in cool, damp, stagnant conditions. More likely in winter and cooler times of year. Remove all diseased parts and burn. Spray with systemic fungicide (benomyl). Improve conditions: reduce watering, ventilate more when possible.

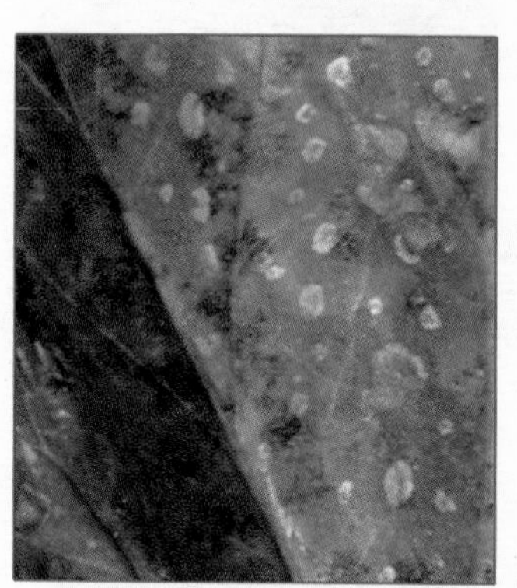

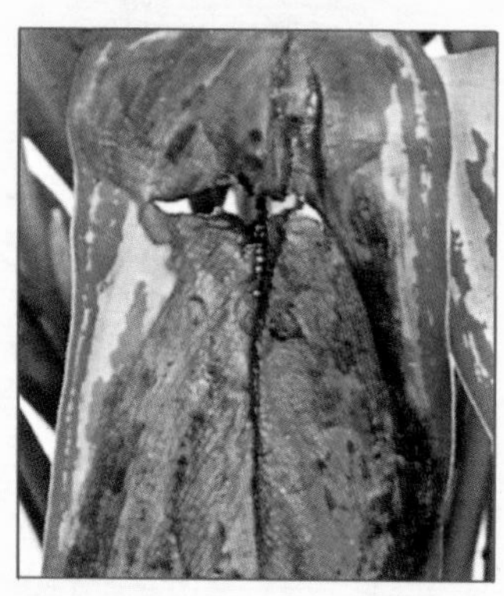

ABOVE Mildew is a fungus disease which is fortunately not all that common.

ABOVE Plants with soft leaves such as the aglaonema (TOP) are particularly prone to Botrytis, another fungal disease.

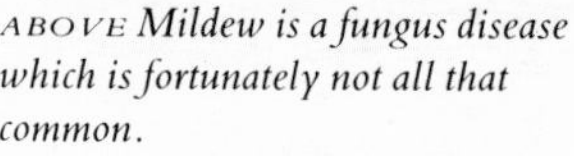

POWDERY MILDEW: Leaves covered with powdery white deposit. Remove worst infected leaves; spray with systemic fungicide or dust with sulphur. Increase ventilation.

SOOTY MOULD: Black fungus growth formed on the honeydew of aphids, scale insects, mealy bug or whitefly. It is both unsightly and stops leaves breathing and photosynthesizing properly. Wipe off with a damp cloth, then control pests producing the honeydew, as advised above.

LEFT Sooty mould grows on the sticky honeydew deposited by aphids and other pests.

RIGHT Dead leaves should be removed regularly (in this case from the base of a cyclamen).

BELOW Cleaning the leaves of Saintpaulia ionantha *(LEFT) and* Ficus robusta *(RIGHT).*

GENERAL HYGIENE

To ensure that your plants thrive and remain in good health it is important to maintain a good standard of hygiene. Remove all dead or withering leaves and flowers promptly so they cannot become starting-points for diseases such as grey mould. Always use proper, sterilized potting composts so as not to introduce diseases or weeds.

Clean the foliage of your plants regularly — perhaps once a month — by wiping the leaves with a damp cloth to remove dust and grime. Rough or hairy leaves should be groomed with a soft brush.

While grooming your plants, trim them back where necessary, tie in wandering growths to a cane, trellis or netting, and provide extra support where it is needed.

Propagating

Those who have only limited time for indoor gardening mostly buy in all their house-plants rather than attempt to raise them from seeds or cuttings. Yet once you have a few plants it is very easy to propagate some of them to create new plants for your collection, to replace old, tired plants, or to provide presents for friends, perhaps in exchange for other species that you want. Propagating plants is fun anyway!

FAVOURABLE CONDITIONS

To coax new roots and shoots from the species of plant you use in propagating, be sure to provide them with the best possible conditions.

Start with proper, sterilized compost, such as peat-based compost with up to half its bulk of sharp sand added (ie peat two parts, sand one) for good drainage and aeration. Keep this moist, but not soggy.

Provide a humid atmosphere so that the cuttings do not lose moisture by covering them with polythene bags or misting them over frequently. (Cacti, succulents and pelargoniums are exceptions, however, and tend to rot if kept humid.)

Provide good light (but not fierce sunshine). Maintain a steady warmth around them of 65-70°F (18-21°C) to stimulate rooting and growth. Use rooting hormone wherever it is likely to be helpful.

Pot rooted cuttings in separate pots of potting compost as soon as they are ready, so that they cannot become starved from lack of food and moisture.

PLANTLETS offer probably the simplest means of increasing your plants. The miniature plants that form naturally on the hanging stems of CHLOROPHYTUM COMOSUM and SAXIFRAGA STOLONIFERA, or around the margins of the succulent leaves of KALANCHOE DAIGREMONTIANA, are eager to root and often bear embryo roots already. Set them in pots of moist compost in warmth (see above) and they should develop into pleasing plants in a few months.

LAYERS are rooted by pinning the trailing stems of ivy (HEDERA), for instance, into pots of compost. When rooted, after a couple of months, they can be severed from their parent and grown separately.

OFFSETS (that is, side growths), formed by bromeliads and many cacti, can be carefully cut from their parent plant and rooted like stem cuttings (see below). As the 'vases' of bromeliads die after flowering, this form of propagation is necessary to allow the plant to survive.

LEAF CUTTINGS are also easy to root. There are several kinds. Wound the main veins on the back of a healthy BEGONIA REX leaf in several places, then pin it or

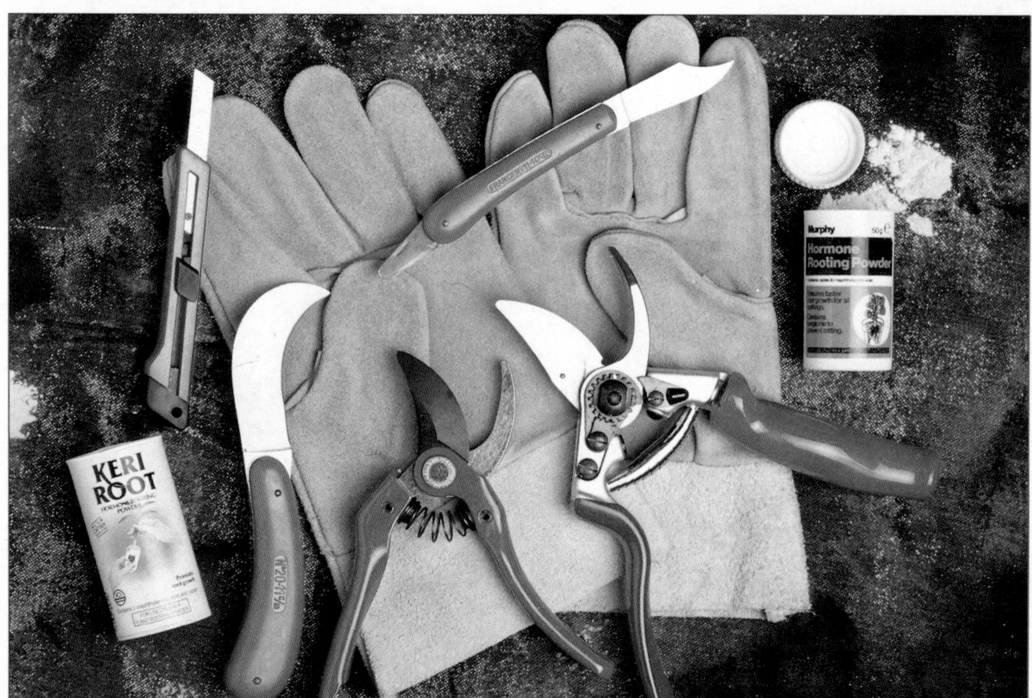

ABOVE *Saintpaulia leaf cutting; include 2in (5cm) of leaf stalk and dip in hormone rooting powder.*

LEFT *Hormone rooting powders, leather gloves, and (from left to right) cutting implements designed for the purpose, which make propagation – and general care – a whole lot easier: scalpel (X-Acto knife), pruning knife, small pruners, budding knife, and secateurs (which are available in left- and right-handed versions).*

weight it to the surface of a tray of moist sandy-peaty compost. After some weeks, and given adequate warmth and moisture, tiny plantlets will grow from the wounds. When well rooted they can be potted off separately.

Saintpaulia leaf cuttings are taken with 2 in (5 cm) of leaf stalk attached. After being treated with rooting hormone, they are then inserted at an angle of 45 degrees in rooting compost, the blade of the leaf just clear of the surface. Within a few weeks, plantlets should develop at soil level.

Leaves of succulent plants such as echeveria and crassulas can also be rooted. Insert the end of each leaf into rooting compost after dusting with rooting hormone; after some weeks each should form a baby plant.

STEM CUTTINGS can be used to increase a wide variety of house-plants. They vary from the fleshy stems of trailing TRADESCANTIA FLUMINENSIS to the cane-like stems of BEGONIA CORALLINA 'Lucerna' and the semi-ripe cuttings taken from pelargoniums (zonal geraniums) in late summer. Treat cactus cuttings similarly but leave them to dry for a couple of days before being inserted. Being prickly, they need handling with gloves or a pad of newspaper.

Main points to ensure success are first to select suitable pieces of plant — stems about 3-5 in (7.5-12.5 cm) long according to the type of plant, thick enough to have the vigour to root, but not so thick and fleshy that they rot. Remove the lower leaves so they are not buried when the cutting is inserted. Cut straight across beneath a leaf joint at the base and dip in hormone rooting powder. Insert to half their depth in suitable compost and keep warm and humid until rooted. Then pot off separately in potting compost. For variations see **A-Z OF PLANTS.**

SEED-RAISING. Home gardeners seldom raise house-plants from seed because most take too long to develop into truly ornamental specimens, and because other methods of propagation (or buying in) are quicker. But it is possible to raise a batch of colourful coleus plants quite easily and cheaply from seeds, and perhaps to attempt some of the seed strains of pelargonium.

Use sterilized seed-sowing compost; firm it moderately in trays or pots, moisten, and allow to drain. Then sow the seeds thinly to avoid overcrowding when they germinate. Cover with a plastic bag, a sheet of glass, or put into a propagator to keep warm and humid. Ventilate occasionally if necessary to prevent stagnant air which could encourage fungus infection. As soon as the seeds germinate, remove the covering, give more air and light — but not so much that the seedlings are chilled or scorched. When they have

LEFT AND BELOW You may feel that raising cacti from seed is too much trouble; on the other hand, with a little success, you may be hooked! The cacti (below) have been 'pricked out' (spaced out) to grow on.

developed their first small true leaves and can be handled, lift them carefully and plant them spaced out ('prick out') in trays of potting compost to grow larger. Once they are well rooted with several pairs of leaves, pot them separately.

DIVISION of clump-forming plants like chlorophytum, aspidistra and maranta offers another easy means of increasing your stock. Remove the plant from its pot and pull it apart as carefully as possible to limit damage to its roots, then repot the two or three divisions so made. You may need to cut through the thick rootstock of plants like stromanthe.

AIR LAYERING is a useful way of giving a fresh lease of life to leggy monsteras and FICUS ELASTICA or F. BENJAMINA which have become leggy and unsightly from losing many of their lower leaves. Root the top 2 ft (60 cm) of the plant by first removing a ½ in (1.3 cm) length of bark just beneath a leaf joint where you wish it to root. Treat this wound with rooting hormone, then wrap it around with a wad of moist sphagnum moss to keep it damp and encourage rooting, and seal in a bandage of clear plastic film, secured top and bottom with insulating tape. Within a couple of months roots should be showing through the moss and the rooted top can be severed from the main plant and potted separately. The truncated original plant can generally be pruned back so that it sprouts and forms a new bushy specimen.

Group and Display

One or two well-grown pot plants, shining with health, resting on a window sill, can certainly give enduring pleasure and bring a room to life. But house-plants can do far more for your home than this. Why not be more adventurous and experiment with some of the more unusual ways of displaying them?

Broadly, there are three ways in which you can display plants to greater effect. Firstly try grouping several plants of contrasting shape, habit, coloration and texture in a single container, rather than side by side in separate pots. Secondly, try to grow a few much larger specimen plants in tubs, urns or large pots as bold features in your room. Thirdly, feature at least one of the more unusual forms of display, such as a hanging basket (perhaps of macramé), a bottle garden, a terrarium, a moss pole supporting a glossy evergreen creeper, or even a dead tree branch decorated with bromeliads and jungle cacti. Which you choose depends, of course, on the size of your room, the furnishings, and what light it provides the plants.

Grouping plants together in bowls, troughs, urns or other containers has several advantages. It creates more impressive features than single pot plants scattered about. Then, by choosing a good mixture of plants — an upright dracaena, a trailing ivy and a bushy pilea, for instance — the contrast of shape and coloration serve to accentuate all their pleasing ornamental features. Besides this, plants usually thrive all the more for being grown together in a larger body of moist compost with a steadily humid atmosphere around them.

A further development of this approach is to plant small collections of plants that like similar conditions in miniature gardens. So a large bowl could be planted with a selection of small ferns — pellaea, ASPLENIUM NIDUS, nephrolepis, pteris — in a peaty compost set off by a few 'rocks' for decoration. Or plant some cacti and succulents to form a desert garden — being careful to provide a gritty, well-drained compost and not to overwater them. These naturally need plenty of light.

OPPOSITE *A wickerwork planter with a waterproof plastic liner suits this room setting very well. A selection of plants have been arranged around a Monstera deliciosa and a cabbage palm,* Cordyline indivisa. *The latter is much more resilient than* Cordyline *(often listed as* Dracaena*)* terminalis. *Always bear these differences in mind when choosing plants.*

LEFT *A moss pole is perfect for many ferns and ivies.*

RIGHT Sedum rubrotinctum *thriving in a terrarium; terrariums are suitable for slow growers.*

Large specimen plants — a howea palm, a 5-6 ft (1.5-1.8 m) FICUS BENJAMINA, or a group of three grevilleas — can be used to break the bareness of a length of wall in a room, to hide a supporting pillar, or just as a large and graceful decoration. Several large evergreens 4-5 ft (1.2-1.5 m) high could be disposed to divide a large room into two distinct areas — one for dining, one for sitting, maybe. An alternative form of room divider could be created by training a cissus or rhoicissus creeper over a light wooden trellis.

Hanging baskets filled with ferns or cascading variegated ivies can look highly decorative. But it is essential to keep the compost moist (and at the same time avoid splashing mud and water on your furnishings). Baskets with drip trays are essential indoors.

A moss pole is easily made from a tall cylinder of plastic mesh packed with moist sphagnum moss. This provides support and a rooting medium for plants such as PHILODENDRON SCANDENS and many of the ferns and ivies, which root into it, enjoy the moist, humid environment, and are quite happy with the nourishment they receive from the compost in the pot at the base.

Terrariums, like miniature greenhouses of various shapes, are popular and decorative, although the accommodation for plants is rather limited. Keep the plants — which should be evergreen and slow growers — moist but not too wet. Ensure that they get enough light according to their species.

Bottle gardens can be created in carboys, old sweet jars, glass battery cases, aquaria, or other suitable containers. Provide conditions similar to those of a terrarium, and include again slow-growing plants that are not likely to swamp the interior with growth or drop leaves that will soon rot and ruin the display. Make miniature tools on long cane handles to manage a narrow-necked carboy.

Many bromeliads (plants of the pineapple family) are by nature epiphytes (plants that grow on trees), so they and jungle cacti like rhipsalidopsis can look convincing as well as highly decorative if grown in wads of moist sphagnum moss attached to a dead tree branch stripped of its bark. They need little more than misting over with water from a hand sprayer.

SELF-WATERING POTS AND HYDROCULTURE

House-plants are more dependent upon their owners for water than for their other needs, and quickly suffer if not regularly supplied. So it is useful to know two ways by which to avoid the slavery of frequent watering.

Self-watering pots consist of a plastic pot containing the plant and its compost, set within a larger pot which provides a reservoir of water and dilute liquid foods in the base. The plant can draw its requirements from the reservoir, which is replenished through a filler tube as necessary, every few weeks.

Hydroculture works along similar lines, except that the plants grow in containers of baked clay granules, which merely support them physically. They draw all their nourishment from the reservoir in the base of the container.

A wide range of sizes is available in both types of automatic watering pot.

An A to Z of Hardy Houseplants

Aechmea fasciata

also known as A. RHODOCYANEA

BROMELIACEAE ▪ URN PLANT

ABOVE RIGHT Aechmea fasciata *'Variegata'; fasciata means 'banded' in Latin.*

AECHMEA FASCIATA is one of the largest and most handsome of the bromeliads (pineapple family). It forms a bold rosette 2-4 ft (60-120 cm) across of tough, spiny-edged, grey-green leaves, irregularly cross-banded with silver. When mature (3-4 years old), it produces a flower stem from its centre, bearing a 6 in (15 cm) cluster of pink bracts from which pale blue flowers appear briefly. The bracts remain decorative for several months, after which the flower stem dies, followed by the rosette itself. The latter is usually replaced by one or more offsets (young rosettes) which form at the base of the parent plant.

These plants are native to the South American rain forests and are adapted to live in the treetops, forming part of a natural 'roof garden' there. They rely for their water and nourishment entirely upon the rain, rotted vegetation, and the remains of the many small creatures that live or feed in the reservoirs formed by their leaves.

To succeed with these plants, which are not difficult to maintain, imitate their natural conditions as nearly as possible. The main requirement is to keep the central cup topped up with water. Use soft, lime-free water for this. Give the plants good light, adequate warmth (preferably 60°F/15°C or more), and free-draining compost.

CARE

LIGHT AND POSITION

Prefers good sunlight and will not flower unless well lit.

TEMPERATURE

Aechmea prefers 60-75°F (15-24°C) with a humid atmosphere, but will tolerate cooler, drier conditions down to 50°F (10°C).

WATERING

The prime need is for the reservoir at the centre of the leaves to be kept topped up with soft water, as in nature. Keep the compost moist, but allow its surface to dry out between waterings.

FEEDING

To compensate for lack of the nutrients it would receive in the forests, give it a very weak liquid feed about once every two weeks from spring to autumn.

COMPOST

Should resemble the rotted vegetation it would naturally grow in. Equal parts of moss peat, leaf mould and gritty sand make a suitable mixture.

SEASONAL CARE

Mist foliage with water — again lime-free to avoid chalky white marks — while it is in active growth. Stand potted aechmeas on tray or saucer of moist pebbles. Reduce watering and cease feeding during mid-winter period (when light is poor) to give them a rest. Root any offsets in spring in 3 in (7.5 cm) pots of equal-parts peat and sharp sand mixture in warmth (70°F/21°C). Save any roots that have already formed or use rooting hormone. Keep lightly shaded and watered until well rooted.

Aeonium arboreum

CRASSULACEAE ▪ TREE AEONIUM

above *A spectacular specimen of* Aeonium arboreum *grown professionally under glass (foreground); your indoor aeonium is unlikely to grow more than 2 ft 6 in high.*

— CARE —

LIGHT
Good light and sun, or there will be only weak growth.

TEMPERATURE
Warm room temperatures in summer, 60-75°F (15-24°C), but cooler to rest in winter (50-55°F/ 10-13°C).

WATERING
Moderate while growing, only enough to prevent parching.

FEEDING
Liquid feed fortnightly in the growing season.

COMPOST
Mixture of 2 parts soil-based compost and 1 part coarse sand for sharp drainage. Move into larger pot annually in spring if root growth makes this necessary.

PROPAGATION
Root tip cuttings — rosette with 1 in (2.5 cm) of stem — in spring in peat/sand mix after dipping end of stem in hormone rooting powder. Should root within three weeks in 70°F (21°C). Move into normal potting mixture once established.

Aeonium arboreum — unlike most aeoniums, which form succulent ground-hugging rosettes of fleshy leaves — is a taller, branching species, although the 'tree' it forms is unlikely to reach more than 2 ft 6 in (75 cm) high.

Each branch carries a typical aeonium rosette at the end, but the lengthening stems are bare and gaunt-looking. Nonetheless it is an eye-catching plant — far more so in its purple-leaved form 'Atropurpureum', which is quite distinctive by reason of its rich bronzy leaf-colouring.

Agave americana

AGAVACEAE ▪ CENTURY PLANT

—CARE—

LIGHT
Good light and sun always, but avoid sudden changes in light intensity.

TEMPERATURE
Normal room temperatures in summer — 60-75°F (15-24°C), cooler in winter (50-55°F/10-13°C).

WATERING
Moderate during summer, letting the plant partly dry out between waterings; minimum in winter to keep just moist.

FEEDING
Liquid feed fortnightly while it is actively growing.

COMPOST
Soil-based mixture 3 parts, with 1 part coarse sand for sharper drainage.

PROPAGATION
Detach any offsets that form, and root in recommended potting mixture (see above).

AGAVE AMERICANA, the Century Plant from Mexico, is so called because it is said to flower only once in a hundred years. It does take many years to flower, although not a hundred, and the rosette of leaves dies when the flowers fade on its tall inflorescence, which can reach 15 ft (4.5 m) or more in height.

This agave is grown in the home for its handsome spiny-edged blue-green leaves, and as a slow grower can be enjoyed for many years before it grows too large to accommodate. It can eventually reach 6-7 ft (1.8-2.1 m) in height when mature.

There is also a less vigorous-growing variegated form known as 'Marginata' that has creamy margins to its leaves. Both plants are hardy in milder areas once they are acclimatized to living outdoors like the specimen illustrated (variety 'Medio-Picta').

Aglaonema crispum 'Silver Queen'

ARACEAE

CARE

LIGHT
Good but not strong, or its leaves could become scorched.

WATERING
Moderate while in active growth; very little while it is resting for a week or two in midwinter. It should always be moist.

TEMPERATURE
Happy in 65-70°F (18-21°C) but tolerates somewhat lower temperatures for a while if not too wet at the root. Stand pot on moist pebbles to provide humidity around its leaves.

FEEDING
Liquid feed once a month, except in midwinter.

COMPOST
Prefers a soil-based compost and a 5-6 in (12.5-15 cm) pot. Pot on small plants or topdress mature ones when necessary to provide fresh nourishment in spring.

SEASONAL CARE
Propagate in spring when growth is most active. Remove a basal shoot with roots attached and pot in an equal-parts mix of peat and sharp sand. Cover with plastic bag and stand in a warm (70°F/21°C) place in moderate light. Old plants can be divided up and treated similarly. New plants should be well enough rooted in two months.

AGLAONEMA CRISPUM 'Silver Queen' is one of several aglaonemas grown for their ornamental variegated leaves. As members of the arum family, they do form typical arum flowers in summer, but these are small, greenish yellow and insignificant.

'Silver Queen's' leaves are grey-green and silver, of pointed oval shape, and arranged in clusters on the plant's several stems. A young plant is low and bushy but in time, as the old leaves are shed and new ones form at the top, it develops stems 1 ft (30 cm) or more tall, bearing the scars of many fallen leaves and a cluster of leaves at the top.

Its handsome overall grey-green colouring makes it an aristocratic-looking foliage plant, fine for a *jardinière* or decorative basket.

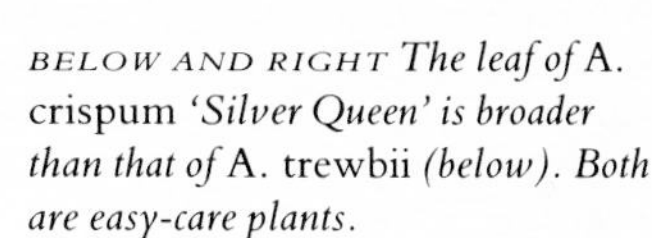

BELOW AND RIGHT The leaf of A. crispum *'Silver Queen' is broader than that of* A. trewbii *(below). Both are easy-care plants.*

Ananas comosus variegatus

BROMELIACEAE ▪ ORNAMENTAL PINEAPPLE

—CARE—

LIGHT
Bright light is essential, particularly to ensure good colour in its variegations and for flowering.

TEMPERATURE
Prefers warmth of 65-75°F (18-24°C) with high humidity, but will tolerate lower temperatures down to 55°F (13°C) and reduced humidity. Stand pot on moist pebbles or plunge in damp peat.

COMPOST
Prefers a soil-based compost free from lime but with extra peat added. The root system is small, so do not overpot. Use a clay pot or the plant could become top-heavy in a plastic pot and fall over.

WATERING
Moderate throughout the year, letting it partly dry out between waterings.

FEEDING
Liquid feed twice a month throughout the year.

SEASONAL CARE
This plant does not have a rest period. Propagate from offsets 4-6 in (10-15 cm) long, removed from the parent with a sharp knife, together with any roots already formed. Pot in 3 in (7.5 cm) pot of equal parts peat and gritty sand; cover with a plastic bag and stand in a warm (70°F/21°C) place that has filtered light. It should root in a couple of months. Then remove bag and water just a little to keep compost moist until strongly rooted.

A. comosus; *in the wild, a terrestrial rather than tree-dwelling bromeliad.*

ANANAS COMOSUS VARIEGATUS is a strikingly decorative form of the cultivated pineapple of which we enjoy the fruits. It is a terrestrial rather than tree-dwelling bromeliad and has arching spiny-edged leaves some 2-3 ft (60-90 cm) long, distinguished by their broad ivory-white margins. The leaves take on an attractive pink flush in bright sunlight.

A shapely and colourful foliage plant, it can also produce a flower stem from the centre of its rosette of leaves when about six years old. This bears colourful pink bracts which remain decorative for some months and can be followed by a small inedible pink pineapple fruit.

Like other bromeliads, its rosette dies after flowering, but offsets should form at its base and can be carefully removed and potted to make new plants.

Anthurium scherzerianum

ARACEAE ▪ FLAMINGO FLOWER

— CARE —

LIGHT
Moderate light, because it is adapted to jungle.

TEMPERATURE
Warm room temperatures all year, preferably 65-75°F (18-24°C), but tolerates down to 55°F (13°C) for short periods.

WATERING
Generous while growing; restrained during midwinter, but maintain high humidity.

FEEDING
Liquid feed fortnightly while it is actively growing.

COMPOST
Peaty and open texture, so equal-parts soil-based mix of peat and coarse sand is ideal.

PROPAGATION
Divide established clumps with several crowns in spring and pot in peat-based mix. Stand in filtered light at 70°F (21°C) to become established.

ANTHURIUM SCHERZERIANUM is a gaudy plant of the arum family, originally found in Central America. Not surprisingly, therefore, it loves warmth and high humidity. But fortunately, it is less tricky than its larger cousin, A. ANDREANUM, the Painter's Palette, which is really only fully happy in a hot, humid glasshouse.

A. SCHERZERIANUM makes a compact plant some 18 in (45 cm) tall with dark, glossy-green spear-shaped leaves from among which rise its flowering stems, each bearing a brilliant scarlet spathe 3-4 in (7.5-10 cm) long, from which in turn protrudes the spadix, the tail-like organ that carries the flowers. This is orange-red and curled like a pig's tail. These spathes remain decorative for many weeks, earning the plant's keep as part of the home decorations.

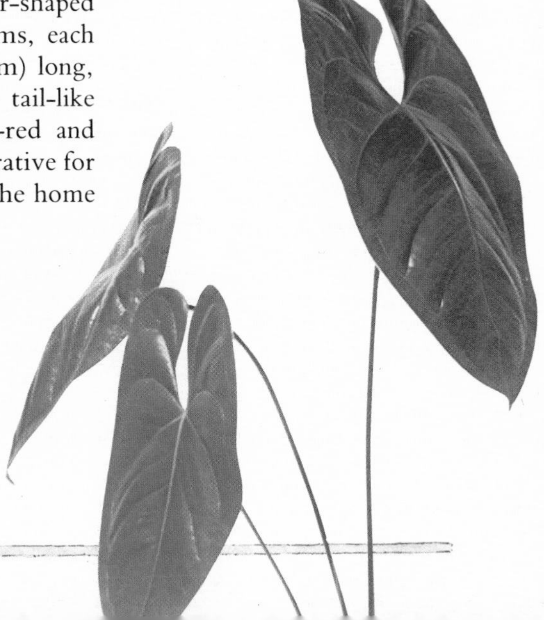

Aphelandra squarrosa louisae

ACANTHACEAE ▪ ZEBRA PLANT

CARE

LIGHT
Give APHELANDRA good but not fierce light.

TEMPERATURE
Enjoys warmth of 65-75°F (18-24°C) in summer, with high humidity provided by standing on a saucer of moist pebbles or frequent misting over. Keep cooler (55-65°F/13-18°C) during its short midwinter rest period, when light is poor.

WATERING
Give enough water to keep the compost really moist all the time the plant is in active growth. Limit supply to keep it barely moist while resting in winter.

FEEDING
Liquid feed this hungry plant regularly every week during its active growth. Give none while resting.

COMPOST
Prefers a soil-based compost with extra peat added. Move into slightly larger pot each spring if pot is filled with roots. After flowering, a plant should be repotted in spring, gently removing most of the old compost and using fresh to provide more nutriment. Cut the plant back to its lowest pair of vigorous leaves, after which it is likely to branch and form a bushy plant.

SEASONAL CARE
Look out for mealy bugs, scale insects and aphids, particularly on succulent young growth in spring.
Root 3 in (7.5 cm) long stem tip cuttings in soil-based-plus-peat mixture in small pot covered with plastic bag and stand in filtered light in a warm (70°F/21°C) place. Takes 6-8 weeks to root.

APHELANDRA SQUARROSA takes its common name of zebra plant from the prominent ivory-white veins on its glossy dark-green leaves. This tropical foliage plant grows about 1 ft (30 cm) high and forms a 5-6 in (12.5-15 cm) tall flower spike in spring consisting of rows of angular yellow bracts from which appear short-lived yellow flowers. The spike of bracts remains attractive for some weeks, but later turns green and should then be removed.

Because they are difficult plants to get to flower, they are generally bought in flower, and afterward kept as striking foliage plants. They are, however, resilient and fairly easy to please. A. SQUARROSA LOUISAE is a selected form more compact and suitable for pots than the species itself.

Aporocactus flagelliformis

CACTACEAE ▪ RAT'S TAIL CACTUS

—CARE—

LIGHT
Good but filtered light. Fierce sun will shrivel its stems.

TEMPERATURE
Warm room temperatures in summer, 60-75°F (15-24°C); cooler in winter, 45-55°F (7-13°C).

WATERING
Generous to keep compost moist while actively growing. Only enough to keep just moist in winter.

FEEDING
Give fortnightly high potash feed while it is in active growth, to improve flowering.

COMPOST
Prefers mix of 2 parts soil-based with 1 part peat-based mixture. Revitalize plants each spring by removing as much old compost as possible and repotting in fresh.

PROPAGATION
Root 6 in (15 cm) tip cuttings in spring in the recommended potting mixture. Let cuttings dry for three days before insertion. They should root in 4-6 weeks.

APOROCACTUS FLAGELLIFORMIS, from Mexico, gets its familiar name from its long, pendant, whipcord-like ribbed stems. These can reach a length of as much as 4-5 ft (1.2-1.5 m) after many years' growth. Its pendulous growth fits it particularly for planting in a hanging basket, a pot suspended on wires, or one stood on a shelf over which its stems can hang freely. The plant is a remarkable sight for some weeks in spring when its stems overflow with dozens of 2 in (5 cm) long gaudy crimson-pink flowers.

This cactus has a quite distinct habitat. Most definitely not a desert cactus, it is not a tree-dweller either (like schlumbergera or epiphyllum). It grows in rock crevices in rotted vegetation and is used to the shade of nearby trees. Generally its needs, therefore, are not dissimilar to those of the tree-dwellers.

Although exotic in appearance, it is a fairly easy plant to manage — but beware its spines if it is hanging overhead. Secure any pot standing on a shelf, or its lengthening stems could become heavy enough to overbalance it.

Araucaria heterophylla

ARAUCARIACEAE ▪ NORFOLK ISLAND PINE

—CARE—

LIGHT
Quite good light, although not fierce sun. In shade it sheds its needles.

TEMPERATURE
Happy between a temperate 45°F (7°C) and a warm 75°F (24°C).

WATERING
Plenty while in active growth from spring to autumn, watering often enough to keep it moist but not soggy. Water moderately during the winter rest period so it is just nicely moist.

FEEDING
Liquid feed twice a month from spring to autumn.

OTHER CARE
Propagated commercially from seed or from cuttings, but this is too demanding for the home gardener.

ARAUCARIA HETEROPHYLLA (or A. EXCELSA) is by nature a tall-growing conifer from Norfolk Island (east of Australia) that can reach 200 ft (60 m) high. It is a relative of the monkey puzzle tree. But while young it can make a pleasant Christmas-tree-like foliage plant which grows only 6 in (15 cm) a year. Obtain it when 1½ ft (45 cm) high and keep it until it is 5 ft (1.5 m), and it can be enjoyed for perhaps seven years.

Its branches are formed in tiers. Fresh growth is made at the top in spring. The lowest tier dies off after several years, leaving the woody trunk visible. A very tolerant plant, provided that it does not dry out.

Asparagus densiflorus 'Sprengeri'

LILIACEAE ▪ ASPARAGUS FERN

—CARE—

LIGHT
Good light, although not fierce sun.

TEMPERATURE
Warm room temperatures, 60-75°F (15-24°C), with a minimum of 55°F (13°C).

WATERING
Generous in summer to keep really moist. Only enough to keep just moist in winter.

FEEDING
Liquid feed fortnightly while it is actively growing.

COMPOST
Soil-based mixture with a little extra peat to improve porosity.

PROPAGATION
Vigorous clumps can be divided in spring. Raising from seeds is too slow to be worth while.

ASPARAGUS DENSIFLORUS 'Sprengeri' is the most resilient of several kinds of so-called asparagus fern grown indoors for their pleasant feathery foliage. For they are not, in fact, ferns at all, but members of the lily family and close cousins of the asparagus eaten as a luxury vegetable.

'Sprengeri' forms long trailing stems up to 3 ft (90 cm) long clothed in fresh green leaflets. It is at its best in a hanging basket from which it can cascade freely, but also makes a good foliage pot plant or a useful member of a mixed group of plants. It is undemanding, provided that its simple needs for warmth and adequate water are met. When potting, allow for expansion of its tuberous roots.

Aspidistra elatior

LILIACEAE ■ CAST-IRON PLANT

CARE

LIGHT
Moderately good light best. Deep shade does not produce the best results. 'Variegata' needs good light.

TEMPERATURE
Tolerates a wide range of temperatures, 45-80°F (7-27°C).

WATERING
Moderate throughout year, partly drying out between waterings. Overwatering harms foliage.

FEEDING
Liquid feed fortnightly while it is actively growing.

COMPOST
Soil-based mixture. Only repot when essential, for these plants do best when undisturbed.

PROPAGATION
By division of strong-growing clumps. Pot well-rooted pieces of rhizome with two or three leaves apiece. Set several together in one pot for a worthwhile display.

ASPIDISTRA ELATIOR, with its inescapable Victorian associations, does indeed have a cast-iron constitution. In that era it was able to sit philosophically on the piano in poor light, hardly affected by the various fumes that often polluted the air, nor by occasional lack of water.

But why have a long-suffering plant when you can enjoy a handsome one by treating it a little more considerately? Aspidistra makes a handsome and shapely foliage plant with glossy green leaves; it looks especially fine in an ornamental *jardinière*.

Mature plants form their flowers at soil level among the leaf stalks. These are dull purple and most intriguing. If you wish for a more exciting plant, grow the form 'Variegata' that has creamy white stripes running the length of its leaves. This form, however, insists upon better light to retain its colour.

Aspidistra elatior *'Variegata' (right) will not tolerate temperatures below 60°F (16°C), unlike the original greenleaved species (above left); bear in mind such differences when choosing your plants if hardiness is an important factor.*

Asplenium nidus

POLYPODIACEAE ▪ BIRD'S NEST FERN

—CARE—

LIGHT
Moderate light suits it best — never bright light, nor deep shade.

TEMPERATURE
Happy in most heated rooms, provided that temperature does not fall below 60°F (15°C).

WATERING
Keep really moist while it is actively growing, but barely moist during winter rest period. Plunge pot in damp peat or stand on damp pebbles to create humid air around it.

FEEDING
Liquid feed monthly while it is actively growing.

COMPOST
Prefers a mixture of peat, leaf mould and gritty sand in equal parts. As an epiphyte (growing on trees) it makes only a small root system, so do not move into larger pot unless obviously necessary.

PROPAGATION
A. NIDUS forms no offsets or plantlets, and so is raised from spores commercially. This is too difficult for home gardeners.

ASPLENIUM NIDUS is a tropical and sub-tropical fern that grows naturally on trees in the South Pacific and Australia. It is distinct from most ferns in having undivided fronds, more like the leaves of flowering plants, which form a bowl-shaped plant, hence its familiar name of bird's nest fern.

Bought plants may be only 4 in (10 cm) across, but they can in time reach as much as 6 ft (1.8 m) across. New fronds uncurl in typical fern manner from the centre of the rosette and are soft and brittle, but after spreading out fully become tough and leathery. Wipe the fronds of indoor A. NIDUS plants regularly to clean off dust and grime. Provide a very humid atmosphere around the plant in spring and summer, while it is active.

Begonia corallina 'Lucerna'

BEGONIACEAE ▪ SPOTTED ANGEL WING BEGONIA

—CARE—

LIGHT
Good light essential to get full colouring, but not strong light, which could scorch or bleach the leaves.

TEMPERATURE
Ordinary room temperatures (65-75°F/18-24°C) in summer. Lower temperatures during winter rest period, but minimum of 60°F (15°C). Ensure high humidity round plants' foliage by standing on tray of moist pebbles.

WATERING
Moderate during the active growing season, so compost remains moist except for surface ½ in (1.3 cm) which should dry out between waterings. Reduce watering during rest period, keeping compost barely moist. Avoid cool, damp conditions which can encourage powdery mildew.

FEEDING
Liquid feed about twice a month from spring to autumn, while it is actively growing.

COMPOST
Peat-based or a mixture of this and soil-based compost is suitable. Use a shallow container, for the roots do not run deep.

PROPAGATION
Root 3-4 in (7.5-12 cm) long stem cuttings at any time during the active growing season in an equal-parts peat/sand mixture, then repot into a mixture of soil-based mix with extra peat when well rooted and growing away.

BEGONIA CORALLINA 'Lucerna', one of the cane-stemmed begonias from Brazil, is at once an easily pleased plant and highly decorative, both in its foliage and its clusters of coral-pink flowers. It is also very easy to strike plantlets from stem cuttings, so once you possess a plant you can soon make more, to replace exhausted plants or those which have outgrown the space allocated to them.

The elephant's-ear-shaped leaves can be 6 in (15 cm) or more long, bright green with whitish spots above and rich wine-red underneath. They look especially fine when the sun shines through them. The green cane-like stems about ⅓-⅜ in (8-10 mm) thick can grow several feet (about 1 m) tall, but tend to branch if the tips are pinched out. The profuse clusters of flowers form at almost any time during the active growing season, from spring to autumn.

Begonia rex

BEGONIACEAE ▪ REX BEGONIA

BEGONIA REX is the name of a group of hybrids grown for their exceptionally handsome, beautifully coloured and marked leaves. They may flower, but the blossoms are small and insignificant. B. REX grows from a rhizome that extends across the surface of the soil and gives rise to 8-10 in (20-25 cm) long leaves on 8-12 in (20-30 cm) long hairy leafstalks. Leaf colouring can vary from silvery green with dark purple edge to almost black-purple with silver band parallel to the leaf edge. Others are dull crimson with silver spots, or can combine concentric zones of green, silver, red and purple.

Well-grown plants reach about 9 in (22.5 cm) high and 1 ft (30 cm) across. Because the rhizomes are shallow-rooted, they are happiest in shallower half-pots or pans rather than full-depth pots. Their noble appearance makes them especially suitable for growing in ornamental containers of appropriate size and shape, perhaps as a table centrepiece. BEGONIA REX is deciduous, its leaves dying and falling in the poor winter light, but with care it can soon look as attractive the next spring.

CARE

LIGHT

Good light essential to get full colouring, but not strong light, which could scorch or bleach the leaves.

TEMPERATURE

Ordinary room temperatures (65-75°F/18-24°C) in summer. Lower temperatures during winter rest period, but minimum of 60°F (15°C). Ensure high humidity round plants' foliage by standing on tray of moist pebbles.

WATERING

Moderate during the active growing season, so compost remains moist except for surface ½ in (1.3 cm) which should dry out between waterings. Reduce watering during rest period, keeping compost barely moist. Avoid cool, damp conditions which can encourage powdery mildew.

FEEDING

Liquid feed about twice a month from spring to autumn, while it is actively growing.

COMPOST

Peat-based or a mixture of this and soil-based compost is suitable. Use a shallow container, for the roots do not run deep.

PROPAGATION

Best done by means of leaf cuttings. Take a healthy leaf, would the main veins on the back, then pin it down on the surface of a moist peat/sand mixture. Plantlets will form within a month from the wounds, given suitable warmth (70°F/21°C), filtered light, and adequate moisture. (Put in plastic bag or propagator.) Alternatively, ½ in (1.3 cm) squares cut from a healthy leaf can be inserted upright in similar compost and should form new plants from the main veins. When plantlets have several leaves, pot in separate small pots and water moderately until strongly rooted.

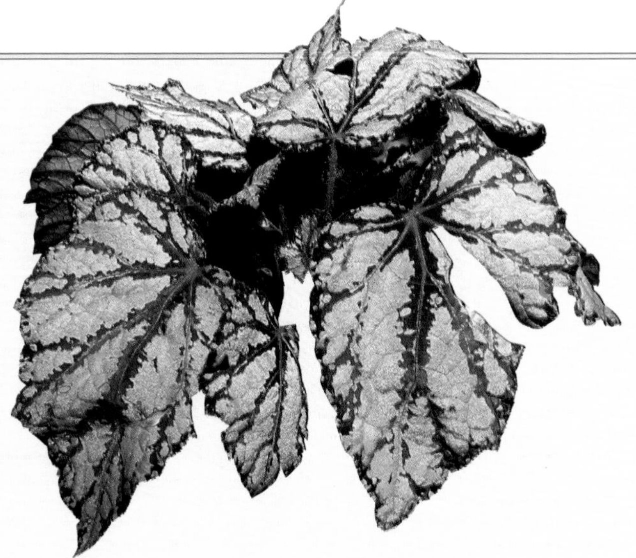

Beloperone guttata

ACANTHACEAE ▪ SHRIMP PLANT

—CARE—

LIGHT
Provide good light with some sun. In shade beloperone becomes straggly and forms no shrimps.

TEMPERATURE
Keep warm but not hot or it will grow weakly. In summer 65-75°F, in winter a few degrees lower, although it has no rest period.

WATERING
Just enough to keep compost moist but allow surface 1 in (2.5 cm) to dry out between waterings.

FEEDING
Liquid feed twice a month while it is actively growing, from late spring to early autumn.

COMPOST
Use 3 parts soil-based compost with 1 part peat added to aid water-holding capacity. Move plant into larger pot each spring, or top dress when already in large (6 in/15 cm) pot.

SEASONAL CARE
Root tip cuttings 2-3 in (5-7.5 cm) long in peat/sand mixture in spring. Cover pots of cuttings with plastic bag; keep in diffused light in a warm (65-70°F/18-21°C) place. Cuttings should root in a couple of months.
Cut older plants back by about one half in spring to keep growth compact.

BELOPERONE GUTTATA, the intriguing Shrimp Plant, does produce very authentic-looking shrimps. In fact, I have known a cat who ate them as fast as the plant produced them! Fortunately the flowering season is long — three-quarters of the year — so this plant remains interesting for months, although its foliage is unimpressive.

The 4-5 in (10-12.5 cm) long 'shrimps' are formed of overlapping pinkish brown bracts, from which tiny white flowers briefly appear.

A neat, compact plant when bought from a florist or nursery, this beloperone is by nature a rather straggly shrub 2-3 ft (60-90 cm) high, so it must be kept to shape and size. Cut away one third to one half of its top growth in spring and pinch any wayward shoots later as necessary.

Billbergia nutans

BROMELIACEAE ▪ QUEEN'S TEARS (OR FRIENDSHIP PLANT)

CARE

LIGHT
Enjoys good light and needs some direct sunlight regularly if to flower each year. There is no definite flowering season, so blooms can appear from spring to early autumn.

TEMPERATURE
Very amenable, 45-75°F (7-24°C).

WATERING
Keep the compost in which they are growing moist all the time, because there is no rest period in winter, but leave the surface to dry between waterings. Use soft, lime-free water or rainwater.

FEEDING
Liquid feed about twice a month.

COMPOST
Use equal parts of lime-free soil-based compost and peat, and smallish pots for the size of the plant because their root systems are small. Move into larger pot in spring when it becomes essential. It may prove necessary to use a clay pot to prevent this rather top-heavy plant from falling over.

PROPAGATION
Easy from offsets in spring, but they must be 4-6 in (10-15 cm) tall and maturing with roots forming or about to form. Insert ½-¾ in (1.3-1.8 cm) deep in bromeliad potting mix and support with a cane. Stand in a moderately light place and water sparingly until well rooted, as occurs usually after a couple of months.

Billbergia nutans is a particularly tough easily-managed terrestrial bromeliad from Brazil and Argentina, which forms 12-14 in (30-35 cm) long flowering stems clothed in 3 in (7.5 cm) long pink bracts. From these hang nodding clusters of dainty flowers, whose green petals have a rich blue margin and a pink calyx, also with a blue margin. Although it is less showy than many of the bromeliads, its ease of cultivation makes it particularly popular.

Its arching grey-green thorny-edged leaves, 1 ft (30 cm) or more long, are tubular at the base and form clustered rosettes of growth. A plant is likely to need a larger pot every second year, and it provides plenty of offsets that can be carefully removed and potted separately in order to form new plants.

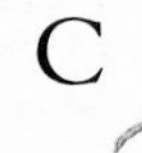

Campanula isophylla

CAMPANULACEAE ▪ ITALIAN BELLFLOWER

CARE

LIGHT
Good light, although not fierce sun.

TEMPERATURE
Normal room temperatures in summer (60-75°F/15-24°C); 45-50°F (7-10°C) in winter while resting. Minimum of 45°F (7°C).

WATERING
Enough to keep compost moist in summer; less in winter to keep barely moist.

FEEDING
Liquid feed fortnightly during active growth.

PROPAGATION
Root 2 in (5 cm) long tip cuttings in spring in peat/sand mix after treating with rooting hormone. Cover with plastic bag. Should root within three weeks.

CAMPANULA ISOPHYLLA was a traditional favourite for a country cottage windowsill. These days, however, as a trailing plant, it is more often displayed in a hanging basket where it is visually at its best, 15-24 in (37.5-60 cm) across. It is a gorgeous china-blue — unless you happen to have chosen the equally attractive and floriferous white-flowered form.

This campanula's flowers open soon after midsummer and — if the plant is well cared for and spent blooms are quickly nipped off to stop the plant setting seeds — it will keep flowering until autumn. Given enough light and moisture and moderate warmth, it is easy to please. Stem cuttings root easily too, so there is no problem in keeping a succession of plants going.

RIGHT *The mass of star-shaped white flowers of* C. isophylla *'Alba', ideal for display in a hanging basket.*

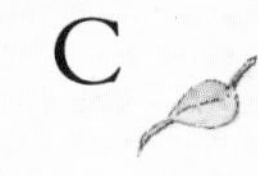

Ceropegia woodii

ASCLEPIADACEAE ▪ ROSARY VINE (OR HEARTS ON A STRING)

CEROPEGIA WOODII must be unique among house-plants in that it is at once both a succulent plant and a trailer suitable for a hanging basket. As its familiar names imply, its stringy stems — which can grow 3 ft (90 cm) long, possibly more in favourable places — carry many scattered heart-shaped fleshy leaves, like beads on a rosary. The stems are purple, the leaves dark green and marked silvery white above and purple beneath. The stems and leaves provide the plant's main interest, but small tubular purple flowers in late summer add considerably to the effect.

This ceropegia grows from a tuber which remains on the surface of the compost and may become 1½-2 in (3.8-5 cm) across. Other smaller tubers may form at intervals down its stems and can be used to make new plants. Grow the plant in a small hanging basket or a pot suspended on wires. It is generally quite undemanding, although it must have good light.

CARE

LIGHT
Good light with several hours' sun per day.

TEMPERATURE
Normal warm room temperatures 60-75°F (15-24°C) all year.

WATERING
Abstemiously during active growing season, the barest minimum in winter to avoid wilting.

FEEDING
Liquid feed monthly only while growing strongly.

COMPOST
Soil-based mixture mixed with equal amount of coarse sand or perlite.

PROPAGATION
Remove stem tubers or take stem cuttings in spring or summer. Put tuber on ½ in (1.3 cm) layer of sand covering small pot of recommended potting mix and keep just moist. It forms feeding roots and starts to grow shoots within a couple of months. Insert cuttings in similar mixture, allowing some sand to dribble into the holes, and treat as for tubers.

Chamaedorea elegans

PALMAE ▪ PARLOUR PALM

CHAMAEDOREA ELEGANS, the parlour palm, often sold under the name NEANTHE BELLA, is particularly useful in the home because it is shorter in stature than most palms yet still pleasing. It rarely exceeds 3 ft (90 cm) in height and takes several years to reach that stature.

Its leaves, consisting of paired leaflets some 6 in (15 cm) long, vary from 1½ to 2 ft (45 to 60 cm) in length and grow from green woody stems. It often flowers while only 1 ft (30 cm) high, displaying tiny ball-shaped flowers. It is an easy plant to manage, provided that it gets enough moisture and not too much heat or light.

Grow one in a large pot or *jardinière* to provide a vertical accent. Alternatively, while it is small, grow it within a group of lower, more spreading plants. A young plant is even suitable for a bottle garden.

— CARE —

LIGHT
Good but filtered light. Stands some shade but in poor light becomes drawn and weak.

TEMPERATURE
Fairly tolerant, but prefers normal room temperature of 65-75°F (18-24°C) in summer, lower in winter, with a minimum of 55°F (13°C). Keep the air humid around it by misting and by standing it on a saucer of moist pebbles. Leaf tips could brown if the air is too dry, and red spider mites could appear.

WATERING
Give plenty of water during season of active growth, so that compost is always moist. Reduce in winter with longer intervals between waterings so that compost is only just moist.

FEEDING
Give a weak liquid feed monthly during active growth only.

COMPOST
Use a soil-based mix (3 parts) with extra peat (1 part) added to improve porosity and water-holding capacity. Only move this palm into a larger pot when really necessary. Firm it down gently, for its fleshy roots are brittle.

SEASONAL CARE
Mist foliage regularly when air is dry to discourage red spider mite. If the mite is present, leaflets turn yellow and mottled. This plant cannot be propagated in ordinary home conditions.

Chrysanthemum morifolium

COMPOSITAE ▪ POT CHRYSANTHEMUM

CARE

LIGHT
Good light, but not fierce sun.

TEMPERATURE
Cool, from 50-65°F (10-18°C), or plants wilt and blooms go over quickly.

WATERING
Generous to keep compost moist. Remember that one pot may contain several dwarfed plants, each with its own root system.

FEEDING
As temporary plants they need none.

COMPOST
They need no repotting so this question does not normally arise. If you wish to group several plants, pack moist peat between them.

GENERAL CARE
Propagation is out of the question. Just buy new plants. Make sure these are showing at least some colour in their flower buds, or they may fail to open. Watch for pests, notably aphids, whitefly and red spider mite.

Pot chrysanthemums are now among the most popular of all indoor flowering plants. They must be accepted as temporary plants only, however, because after they have flowered it is not possible to keep them and to get them to flower in the same way the next season. Their period of beauty lasts from six to eight weeks — and that is what we must be satisfied with.

They are now available every month of the year, thanks to the use of dwarfing chemicals and to the manipulation of 'daylight hours' by the nurserymen who grow them. It is relatively simple thus to replace spent plants with new ones already showing colour in their buds to give a further period of beauty.

The natural height of these plants is 3-4 ft (0.9-1.2 m), a height to which they revert if planted outdoors after flowering. They are raised by setting six or so rooted cuttings around the rim of a pot, treating them with dwarfing chemicals to keep them about 1 ft (30 cm) high, and encouraging them to form flower buds by blacking out the glasshouse for several hours a day (because they naturally bloom in the short days of autumn).

Their main requirements in the home are good light, moderate warmth (in too much heat their blooms fade quickly), and enough water to keep their compost moist, although not soggy. Their blooms may be white, yellow, bronze, pink or orange.

ABOVE *The 'Charm' hybrid will only flower in the autumn, and is thus a less attractive buy than the new pot chrysanthemums on offer. Remember that with such flowering plants you must be ruthless: the only thing to do with them when their flowers die is to get another plant.*

Cissus antarctica

VITACEAE ▪ KANGAROO VINE

CARE

LIGHT

Prefers bright though not fierce sunlight, which can scorch its tender leaves. Tolerates shadier places.

TEMPERATURE

Likes it warm (65-70°F/18-21°C) for best growth, with a midwinter rest period at 55°F (13°C), but tolerates lower temperatures (to 55°F/13°C) in which it grows less vigorously.

WATERING

Moderate during active growth, whenever drying surface of compost shows the need. Give a minimum during rest period to stop it drying out.

FEEDING

Liquid feed twice a month from spring to autumn.

COMPOST

Use a soil-based mixture. Pot on into a slightly larger pot each spring until in final 8 or 10 in (20 or 25 cm) pot, when it should be top dressed instead.

SEASONAL CARE

Give a rest period of one to two months in midwinter while light is poor, reducing watering and ceasing to feed. Propagate from 3-6 in (7.5-15 cm) long tip cuttings in spring. Remove lower leaves, trim beneath a leaf joint, dip in hormone rooting powder and insert in 3 in (7.5 cm) pot of equal-parts peat and sharp sand. Cover it with a plastic bag and stand it in moderate light in a warm (70°F/21°C) place. Cuttings should root within two months, when the bag can be removed and watering gradually increased.
CISSUS ANTARCTICA may be attacked by red spider mite if the room's atmosphere is dry. Mist foliage regularly with water where possible from spring to autumn. Spray with insecticide if mites are noticed — usually on backs of leaves.

CISSUS ANTARCTICA is a vigorous, handsome climbing plant that clings by its tendrils as it goes. A close relative of the grape vine, it is valued for its shiny, evergreen, oval, pointed leaves 3-4 in (7.5-10 cm) long, and for its tolerance of a wide range of room conditions. Grow it on netting or a trellis to decorate a wall, or in a large pot as a trailer, or in a hanging basket (where it will need some pinching back to keep it more compact). It can also be used to form a natural room divider by training it over a suitable support.

Each stem can make up to 2 ft (60 cm) of fresh growth in a year. Where necessary, trim back the growth to keep the plant within its allotted space and to prevent its becoming too rangy.

Clivia miniata

AMARYLLIDACEAE ▪ KAFFIR LILY

CARE

LIGHT

Give bright light with some sun, but neither scorching sun nor shade, which can stop flowering.

TEMPERATURE

It is happy in a warm room at 60-75°F (15-24°C) in summer, but needs a cooler early winter rest period of about two months (45-50°F/7-10°C) to gain strength for flowering.

WATERING

Give plenty during active growth to keep compost moist and fleshy roots plump. Give the bare minimum during the winter rest period.

FEEDING

Liquid feed twice a month during season of active growth, starting when flower stems are half their eventual height.

COMPOST

Use soil-based potting compost. Clivias flower best when pot-bound, so only repot when essential, every third year or so. In other years revitalize plant in early spring by top dressing with fresh compost after scraping away old. Take care not to damage fleshy surface roots.

Use a clay pot because the plant can become top-heavy in a plastic one and in any case its expanding roots may burst a flimsy pot. When potting in a larger pot, leave 2 in (5 cm) space above rootball because root growth tends to push it upwards out of the pot.

PROPAGATION

Remove rooted offsets from parent plant in spring after flowering and pot first in peat/sand mix until well established. Later put it into soil-based mixture. Sever offset carefully where it joins its parent. Old plants can be divided up and the pieces potted separately. Avoid root damage as far as possible.

CLIVIA MINIATA, the cheerful orange-flowered Kaffir lily from South Africa, is a valuable and remarkably good-tempered flowering houseplant that should bring its owner pleasure for a number of years with minimum care. Its main demands are for adequate light and a winter rest period.

Apart from its rich colourings — it has a dozen or more yellow-throated orange trumpets in each cluster — its virtues are its early spring flowering and its ease of propagation from offsets. Its dark-green strap-shaped leaves, reminiscent of leeks but thicker and fleshier, form an excellent background for the orange blooms.

Coleus blumei

LABIATAE ▪ FLAME NETTLE (OR PAINTED NETTLE)

— CARE —

LIGHT
Give bright light, with some direct sun, to ensure rich colouring and compact growth.

TEMPERATURE
Keep them warm, 60-75°F (15-24°C), and humid in higher temperatures. If the plant is kept much cooler the lower leaves are likely to fall.

WATERING
As often as necessary to keep the compost really moist to sustain growth. If they go short they quickly wilt and lose leaves. Mist foliage regularly in hot dry rooms to deter red spider mite, which can attack these plants.

FEEDING
Liquid feed twice a month to keep growing strongly.

COMPOST
Use a soil-based compost and move into larger pots as soon as existing ones are filled with roots — perhaps three times in a season.

PROPAGATION
Stem tip cuttings 2-3 in (5-7.5cm) long root easily in 70°F (21°C) in potting compost or even in water and serve to make extra plants during the season or to overwinter if conditions are ideal. (Poor light and cool temperatures make this difficult.) Seed-raising by normal technique is simple in temperatures 65-70°F (18-21°C). Seedlings take a week or two to show their full coloration.

COLEUS BLUMEI is a gaudy tropical plant grown for its brightly-coloured richly-patterned leaves. Although it is a shrubby perennial by nature, in temperate zones it is treated as an annual because the plant finds it difficult to overwinter due to inadequate light and to low temperatures. It does produce spikes of pale blue flowers, but these are rather insignificant and detract from the foliage effect, and so are best removed.

It is easiest to start with 2-3 in (5-7.5 cm) seedlings bought from a florist or nursery in spring, although it is possible to raise some from seeds of which there are now some fine selected strains. Cuttings from existing plants root quite easily in warm conditions, at about 70°F (21°C).

These are vigorous plants that demand plenty of food, water and bright light while in active growth. They need larger pots several times in a season, and also require pinching back to keep them a neat shape.

Grow them as single specimens, up to 2 ft (60 cm) tall, several together with variously coloured leaves, or to enliven displays of evergreen foliage plants — provided that they can get enough light.

Crassulas

CRASSULACEAE

CRASSULAS form one of the most important genera of succulent plants. All have thick fleshy leaves — CRASSUS being the Latin word for 'thick' — but vary considerably in habit of growth.

CRASSULA ARGENTEA, the Jade Plant, forms a branched tree-like plant up to 3 ft (90 cm) or more tall, with rich dark-green glossy-surfaced leaves. Although grown primarily for its foliage and general shape, this plant does flower, with clusters of tiny star-shaped white or blush-pink flowers in winter on mature plants.

CRASSULA FALCATA is often known as the Propeller Plant from the shape of its grey-blue leaves, which are somewhat twisted and can be as much as 7 in (17.5 cm) long. This is a sprawling, bushy plant by nature, but the young plant for a long time forms just a single upright stem. Its bright scarlet flowers are quite showy and open in summer. They contrast strikingly with the blue cast of the leaves.

ABOVE Crassula argentea.

RIGHT The twisted bluish leaves of Crassula falcata.

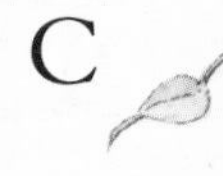

Crassulas

CRASSULACEAE

— CARE —

LIGHT
Must have good light and plenty of sun.

TEMPERATURE
Warm room temperatures, 60-75°F (15-24°C) in summer. Cooler in winter (45-55°F/7-13°C).

WATERING
Moderate in summer to keep moist. Little in winter to keep barely damp.

FEEDING
Liquid feed fortnightly while growing.

COMPOST
Soil-based mixture (3 parts) with coarse sand (1 part). Only move to larger pot when essential.

PROPAGATION
Leaves root in recommended potting mixture in spring/summer. Or root 3 in (7.5 cm) stem cuttings in moist peat/sand mixture in spring.

Cryptanthus bivittatus

BROMELIACEAE ▪ EARTH STAR

—CARE—

LIGHT
Good light all year round to ensure good leaf colour.

TEMPERATURE
Warm room temperature of 60-75°F (15-24°C) with humid atmosphere provided by standing on a tray of moist pebbles.

WATERING
Only enough to keep just moist.

FEEDING
Unnecessary but could foliar-feed occasionally while in active growth.

COMPOST
Use peat-based potting mixture with some coarse sand or perlite to aid drainage, in small pot or half-pot. Leave undisturbed until it needs dividing.

PROPAGATION
From offsets in spring in small pots of equal-parts sand and peat enclosed in plastic bag in warm place in diffused light. It takes several months to root.

ABOVE Cryptanthus bivittatus.

BELOW Cryptanthus bromelioides.

LEFT A massive Crassula argentea.

CRYPTANTHUS BIVITTATUS is about the smallest of the bromeliads (pineapple family) grown ornamentally. It is a terrestrial species that grows in rock crevices or on fallen trees, and its small root system is used almost entirely to anchor it rather than for absorbing its food.

It forms rosettes some 6 in (15 cm) across; the prickly-edged leaves have longitudinal stripes in green and various shades of pink, making it quite a decorative plant. It spreads by means of offsets, but its flowers are of no ornamental value.

It is small enough to be suitable for a bottle garden or other small grouping of plants; alternatively, it could be grown like an epiphyte in moss on a branch.

Desert Cacti

Echinocactus grusonii

Chamaecereus sylvestrii

Echinocereus pectinatus

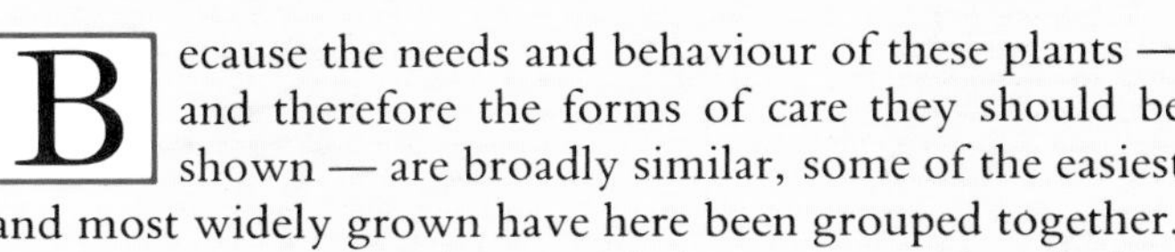

Because the needs and behaviour of these plants — and therefore the forms of care they should be shown — are broadly similar, some of the easiest and most widely grown have here been grouped together.

(Three other popular cacti belong to a quite distinct group, the jungle cacti, which are by nature tree-dwellers and need an altogether moister and somewhat shadier environment to succeed. For these refer to Epiphyllum, Rhipsalidopsis and Schlumbergera elsewhere in this volume. See also Aporocactus, a rock-dwelling species.)

As might be expected, the desert cacti need a minimum of **watering** — but note that they wilt or shrivel if totally neglected. As room plants they should be watered moderately during the growing season, from spring to autumn, then kept barely moist during the poor light conditions and lower temperatures of midwinter.

All are happy in warm rooms at a **temperature** of 60-75°F (15-24°C) in summer, with all the **light** you can give them. In winter allow them to rest at about 45-50°F (7-10°C), while keeping them in as good a light as possible.

As for **compost**, they are generally happy in a soil-based mixture 3 parts, with an extra 1 part of coarse sand to supply the sharp drainage they insist upon.

Propagation is generally from offsets or branches or from seeds (see below).

CHAMAECEREUS SYLVESTRII, the Peanut Cactus, so called from the appearance of its young stems, is a typical, easily-managed small desert cactus for the home. Although small, it is quite a strong grower, quickly filling a 6 in (15 cm) half-pot with side growths, which can be detached to form a ready means of propagation. They are soft green and shaped into a number of longitudinal ribs which carry the areoles and their bunches of whitish spines, and in early summer their scarlet flowers. Each is about 1 in (2.5 cm) wide and lasts for only one day, although a succession of them does keep the plant attractive for several weeks.

ECHINOCACTUS GRUSONII, the Golden Barrel Cactus (sometimes slyly referred to as Mother-in-law's Cushion), is a slow grower unlikely to flower in the home because it needs to grow quite large before doing so. Its main attractions are its symmetrical form — many tubercles aligned as vertical ribs on its low hemispherical shape — and its many golden spines, which contrast handsomely with its dark green body. This cactus is usually reproduced from seeds.

ECHINOCEREUS PECTINATUS, the Hedgehog Cactus, is a neat grower ideally suited for growth on a bright window-sill in a warm room. It takes about six years to reach 4 in (10 cm) in height, after which its single-ribbed stem may branch. It bears clusters of white spines at the areoles on these ribs. Its typical cactus flowers are mauve-pink and up to 3 in (7.5 cm) across, and open throughout summer. A rewarding plant for the little attention it demands.

ECHINOPSIS MULTIPLEX, the Sea Urchin Cactus, again named from the shape of its body, is pale green and has a dozen or more vertical ribs that carry the areoles and clusters of brown spines. Its pale pink flowers are larger than those of many other species — up to 5 in (12.5 cm) across — but are night-flowering, opening a half-hour after dusk.

Desert Cacti

If this habit is frustrating for you, you could grow one of the hybrids made between this and the genus Lobivia. These have peach, orange or red flowers which open during daylight.

GYMNOCALYCIUM QUEHLIANUM, the Rose-plaid Cactus, is of flattened globular shape, growing slowly 5 in (12.5 cm) across but only 2 in (5 cm) high. In summer it opens white flowers 2-3 in (5-7.5 cm) across tinged with red in the centre. Other species of gymnocalycium have red or yellow flowers.

LOBIVIA HERTRICHIANA, the Cob Cactus, takes its Latin generic name from its native country, Bolivia, of which it is an anagram. A relatively small plant that has a globular ribbed body, it forms many offsets, valuable for propagation, and flowers quite prolifically in early summer. Its blooms are some 2 in (5 cm) across and somewhat taller than this. Although each bloom lasts only a day, the display continues for several weeks.

MAMMILLARIA BOCASANA is known as the Snowball Cactus, or the Powder-Puff, so dense is its covering of hairlike white spines. Not all mammillarias are easy to grow, but this one is trouble-free and rewards its grower with an expanding clump of 2 in (5 cm) globes which yield yellow flowers in spring. About ¾ in (1.9 cm) long and ⅓ in (0.8 cm) across, these are not large, but are showy when a number open together. Other mammillaria species provide white or red flowers. Mammillarias are reproduced from seeds or from offsets in spring.

OPUNTIA MICRODASYS, Bunny Ears or Prickly Pear, the latter name referring to the thorny fruits that form on the margins of its pads on mature plants in suitable conditions, is for most people the most typical cactus

Desert Cacti

shape, familiar from Western films. It is formed of oval pads, the surfaces of which are covered with clusters of golden bristles, known as glochids. These are hooked and easily penetrate the skin, so handle with care!

O. MICRODASYS rarely blooms and never fruits in the home, but is valued for its fascinating shape. Its pads are about 3 in by 2 in (7.5 cm by 5 cm) and the plant reaches about 1 ft (30 cm) after several years' growth. It is a great sun-lover, so give it a sunny windowsill and an outdoor holiday in summer.

LEFT Gymnocalycium quelhianum.

TOP LEFT Echinopsis multiplex *'Gay Glory'*.

TOP RIGHT Mammillaria bocasana *'Multilanata'*.

ABOVE Rebutia minuscula.

REBUTIA MINUSCULA, the Crown Cactus (or Mexican Sunball), and several related species of rebutia, are especially rewarding for the home gardener because they are small and easy to accommodate on a sunny windowsill, and are attractive in flower. They bloom early in their lives and increase quite rapidly by forming offsets.

The stems of **R. MINUSCULA** are about 2 in (5 cm) across, almost spherical, and formed of rows of tubercles, each of which carries an areole, the point from which spines and flowers develop. Its flowers are pale red — red in the form GRANDIFLORA, violet in VIOLACIFLORA — and open in late spring. Each bloom lasts about three days, but the succession continues for several weeks.

TRICHOCEREUS SPACHIANUS, sometimes known as Golden Column or the White Torch Cactus, forms a single erect column of vertically-ribbed growth until it reaches 4 ft (1.2 m) or more tall, when it branches from the base. It is grown primarily for its shape, for white trumpet-shaped flowers appear only at the tops of mature plants. It is a comparatively slow grower, taking some seven years to reach 1 ft (30 cm) tall. It is generally propagated from seeds, although it is possible to root a basal branch if one can be spared.

Dieffenbachia maculạta

ARACEAE ▪ DUMB CANE

— CARE —

LIGHT
Moderate in summer. Strong sun can fade leaf colouring. Good light in winter.

TEMPERATURE
Warm room temperatures, 65-80°F (18-27°C), with a minimum of 60°F (15°C), below which leaves may turn brown or drop. Provide high humidity by standing on tray of moist pebbles.

WATERING
Moderate in summer to keep compost moist; let the plant partly dry out between waterings. Keep barely moist in winter if temperature is lowered.

FEEDING
Liquid feed fortnightly while actively growing.

COMPOST
Soil-based mixture with perhaps a little extra peat to maintain porous texture. Move plants into larger pots annually in spring if development justifies.

PROPAGATION
Root a tip cutting 4-6 in (10-15 cm) long in peat/sand mixture in spring in 70-75°F (21-24°C). Remove lower leaves; cut across beneath a leaf joint, dip in hormone rooting powder, insert, then cover with a plastic bag or put in a propagator. (The beheaded stem should produce side shoots.) Alternatively, root sections of stem (cane cuttings) 2-3 in (5-7.5 cm) long, each with one leaf bud. Lay horizontally in surface of peat/sand compost to root in the same as tip cuttings.

DIEFFENBACHIA MACULATA, also called D. PICTA, is a highly decorative foliage plant from Central and South America. Dieffenbachias as a group need high temperatures and high humidity to thrive — particularly some of the variegated forms, which are most treasured for indoor decoration. But fortunately D. MACULATA tolerates somewhat cooler, less humid conditions in the home. It does not, however, withstand any degree of neglect.

It forms a single cane-like stem some 3-5 ft (0.9-1.5 m) tall, which carries its large downward-arching leaves. These are large — some 10 in (25 cm) long and 2½ in (6.3 cm) wide on 4-5 in (10-12.5 cm) stalks — and so when attractively coloured can be very showy. D. MACULATA's green leaves are heavily spotted with white between the leaf veins.

Choicer forms that demand a more jungle-like atmosphere include 'Rudolph Roers', on which mature leaves are almost entirely yellow but for a green edge and central vein. As members of the arum family, mature plants may form typical spathes, each enclosing a flower-bearing spadix, but these are not of any great significance.

The strange familiar name of this plant is accounted for by its poisonous sap, which can cause serious mouth and throat problems. Always wash your hands after taking cuttings from this plant.

Dracaena marginata 'Tricolor'

AGAVACEAE ▪ MADAGASCAR DRAGON TREE

DRACAENA MARGINATA 'Tricolor' is a particularly neat and attractive form of Dragon Tree; it has many gracefully arching leaves ½ in (1.3 cm) wide and about 2 ft (60 cm) long growing from a tall cane-like stem. Whereas D. MARGINATA has green leaves with a narrow red border, 'Tricolor' has in addition a cream band between the other two colours — a considerable improvement for room decoration, yet it is no more difficult to grow.

This is a single-stemmed plant that can grow up to 8 ft (2.4 m) high — but most people do not let it reach that height. When yours becomes too tall, either discard it and buy another, or alternatively, air layer the stem about 2 ft (60 cm) from the top and when well rooted pot the new, much shorter plant.

—CARE—

LIGHT
Good light, but not full sun.

TEMPERATURE
Warm room temperatures, 65-75°F (18-24°C); only an occasional fall to lower level is tolerated. Leaves fall if the plant is chilled. Keep atmosphere humid by standing the pot on a tray of moist pebbles.

WATERING
Generous to keep compost moist while actively growing. Just enough to keep moist during midwinter rest period.

FEEDING
Liquid feed fortnightly while it is actively growing.

COMPOST
Soil-based mixture, perhaps with little extra peat to keep porous. Move into larger pot only when necessary.

PROPAGATION
Root stem cuttings in spring or late summer in moist peat/sand mixture. Cut woody stem with secateurs into 1½-2 in (3.8-5 cm) pieces, each with a growth bud, and be sure to insert right-way-up in compost. Cover with a plastic bag or put in a propagator, where they should root within six weeks.

Echeveria elegans

CRASSULACEAE ▪ MEXICAN GEM

CARE

LIGHT
Revels in full light, even strong sun. Inadequate light weakens the plant so that growth is less compact.

TEMPERATURE
Normal summer room temperatures suit it (ie 60-75°F/15-25°C). It rests during the midwinter months and should then be kept at 55-60°F (13-15°C) so that growth is not forced.

WATERING
Water with restraint even during active growth, letting the compost partly dry out between waterings, so that growth remains compact. Keep water off the leaves or they could be scorched or rot in strong sun. Give only enough water in winter to prevent shrivelling.

FEEDING
Weak liquid feed about twice a month during the season of active growth.

COMPOST
Use a soil-based mixture (4 parts) with extra gritty sand (1 part) added to improve drainage. Move plants into larger pots in spring as necessary, mature ones every second year. Use shallow pans or half-pots because the roots do not run deep; ensure generous drainage (perhaps through clay shards) in the bottom.

SEASONAL CARE
Inspect carefully at regular intervals in case mealy bugs establish themselves between leaves. Dab with alcohol if found. Propagate from offsets or rosettes detached from parent plant, inserting them in recommended potting mixture surfaced with gritty sand (which aids rooting). Trim away lower leaves and cut back any stem to ¾ in (1.9 cm). Should root readily within 2-3 weeks at about 70°F (21°C) in soft light and slightly moist compost.

ECHEVERIA ELEGANS is a neat, rosette-shaped succulent plant that has fleshy blue-grey leaves covered with a white bloom. It is sometimes planted in floral clocks, but is also useful as a windowsill plant or as part of a mixed grouping of succulents. Although grown primarily for its shape and leaf colour, it does also produce clusters of tubular pink and yellow flowers carried on 10 in (25 cm) high stems in summer.

This echeveria is not unlike the hardy houseleek (sempervivum) in habit, and in the same way sends out creeping stems (stolons) from the base of the rosette which carry offsets (miniature rosettes) that can be detached and rooted (if not already rooted) to increase the owner's stock of the plant.

Epiphyllum 'Ackermannii'

sometimes listed as EPIPHYLLUM ACKERMANNII

CACTACEAE ▪ *ORCHID CACTUS*

CARE

LIGHT
Moderate light, as in its leafy forest environment.

TEMPERATURE
Keep warm: 60-80°F (15- 27°C) all year, if possible. Accompany this with high humidity.

WATERING
Plenty in summer, moderate at other times, except a minimum of water for a three-week rest period after each flowering.

FEEDING
Give high potash feed every fortnight only while flower buds are forming.

COMPOST
Use peat-based mixture 3 parts with 1 part of coarse sand or perlite to aid sharp drainage. Move plants into larger pots in spring; when large, replace exhausted soil with fresh, avoiding root damage as far as possible.

PROPAGATION
A branch about 5 in (12.5 cm) long will root in moist compost in spring or summer. Allow to dry off for a day before insertion. Several cuttings round the rim of a pot make a bolder display of flowers once mature.

EPIPHYLLUM 'Ackermannii' or *Nopalxochia ackermannii* is a garden hybrid rather than a naturally-occurring species, and is a magnificent plant when in flower in spring. One of the epiphytic or tree-dwelling cacti from Brazil, it boasts huge flowers compared with those of Rhipsalidopsis and Schlumbergera. Although by no means of an orchid shape, these blooms are surely as splendid as those of a cattleya orchid.

By nature this cactus grows in rotted vegetation in the crotch of a tree, and hangs downwards. But as a house plant it is normally grown in a large pot and any tendency to droop is corrected by careful staking. Given a basic understanding of its needs — a peaty compost, plenty of warmth, high humidity and moderate watering — it is not a difficult plant. Problems generally arise as a result of the misconception that it is a desert cactus that needs spartan treatment. It then shows its disgust by failing to flower and growing hardly at all.

Euphorbia milii

EUPHORBIACEAE ▪ CROWN OF THORNS

—*CARE*—

LIGHT
All the light and sun you can give it.

TEMPERATURE
Warm room temperatures, 60-75°F (15-24°C) with a minimum of 55°F (13°C) in winter.

WATERING
Enough to keep compost moist in summer, allowing to partly dry out between waterings. A minimum in winter, particularly in lower temperatures.

FEEDING
Liquid feed fortnightly during season of active growth.

COMPOST
Soil-based mixture 2 parts with 1 part of sharp sand for good drainage. Move plants into larger pots, or top dress, in spring.

PROPAGATION
Root 3-4 in (7.5-10 cm) tip cuttings in spring in barely moist peat/sand mix. Dip each cutting in water to staunch the flow of milky latex, then leave to dry for a day before insertion. May take two months to root. Give minimum water to keep slightly moist.

EUPHORBIA MILII is a drought-resistant member of this large genus of plants, which originated in Madagascar. It is grown for its rather bizarre beauty, its thorny shrubby growth, somewhat sparse foliage and tiny bright scarlet 'flowers' (really bracts) like drops of blood.

Such a thorny plant, perhaps 2-3 ft (60-90 cm) high, needs to be treated with respect, so stand it where it cannot be brushed against or cause harm to family or friends. It is best located where a challenging visual feature is required.

Euphorbia pulcherrima

EUPHORBIACEAE ▪ POINSETTIA

—CARE—

LIGHT
Good light, but not fierce sun.

TEMPERATURE
Normal warm room temperatures, 60–70°F (15–21°C); a minimum of 55°F (13°C), below which leaf fall is likely.

WATERING
Moderate to keep compost just moist. Allow to start drying out between waterings, then be generous.

FEEDING
Bought plants need no feeding while in 'flower'. If plants are retained, liquid feed monthly while growing.

COMPOST
Bought plants in peat-based mix, but use soil-based with some extra peat if repotting.

PROPAGATION
Root tip cuttings in moist peat/sand mix in spring, after dipping in water to staunch the flow of white latex.

To encourage the formation of bracts on cuttings or retained plants, give 14 hours per day of total darkness from early autumn for two months. Success cannot be guaranteed, but it is an interesting challenge.

EUPHORBIA PULCHERRIMA is far better known as the Poinsettia, now widely sold as a Christmas pot plant. Its bright scarlet bracts are its main attraction, and remain colourful for about a couple of months. Note that they are not flowers but coloured leaves — the true flowers are relatively small and insignificant. There are also forms with white or pale pink bracts, which can look most effective in some colour-schemes, although the colour is more muted.

This euphorbia is by nature a shrubby plant from Mexico which can grow 4–6 ft (1.2–1.8 m) high. As a pot plant it used to be difficult, losing its leaves at the least shock — such as a chill or shortage of water, but the forms now marketed are far less temperamental and more resilient, and so can be bought with confidence. Nonetheless they are best treated as temporary plants to enjoy over Christmas and in the early weeks of the New Year.

It is possible, but difficult, to persuade a plant to form bracts in its second season; it is frankly easier to buy a new plant. The main requirement is to limit the hours of daylight the plant receives in autumn in order to initiate flowering. Plants from florists are additionally treated with a dwarfing chemical to keep them compact. The effect of the chemical normally wears off after a few months, resulting in a taller, leggier plant.

Fatshedera lizei

ARALIACEAE ▪ TREE IVY

CARE

LIGHT

Give moderate light, but not too much shade or its growth can become drawn and weak. The 'Variegata' form needs better, although not strong, light.

TEMPERATURE

A tolerant plant, happy in 60–75°F (15–24°C) in summer, dropping to 45°F (7°C) if necessary in winter. 'Variegata' must be warmer (60°F/15°C) in winter or it could drop leaves.

WATERING

Moderate watering, allowing the surface compost to dry out between waterings; reduced during its short midwinter rest period. Keep moist at the roots or leaves could fall, but never too wet.

FEEDING

Liquid feed twice a month during the warmer part of the year.

COMPOST

Use soil-based mix with extra one-third part of peat, forming a better reservoir of food and moisture than a purely peat-based mix and making the plant physically more stable. Move into a larger pot in spring or top dress largest plants. Check canes and replace if necessary.

PROPAGATION

Keep watch for aphids, scale insects and red spider mite which could appear, particularly on soft young growth
Roots easily from tip cuttings 3 in (7.5 cm) long taken in spring when growth is active and inserted in a peat/sand mixture, covered with a plastic bag and kept warm (65–70°F/18–21°C) in moderately-lit position. Should root within a month, after which remove cover and start to water discreetly.
Fatshederas can also be air layered. This produces larger young plants.

FATSHEDERA LIZEI, a valuable evergreen foliage plant with shiny green leaves, is remarkable for being a hybrid between two distinct genera, *Fatsia japonica* (see below) and the Irish ivy, *Hedera helix hibernica* (sometimes listed as *H. helix* 'Hibernica' or *H. hibernica*). It successfully combines the best features of both plants — more compact with smaller leaves than the fatsia, and better behaved than the unruly spreading ivy — yet is as tough and as easily-managed as them both.

It makes a tall (3–4 ft/0.9–1.2 m) plant with several stems that need the support of a stout cane, clothed with five-lobed palmate leaves 6–8 in (15–20 cm) across. For an extra striking effect insert two or three plants together and train to a central stake to form a fine tapering column of foliage. There is also a distinctive variegated form marked with white along the leaf margins.

BELOW Fatshedera lizei *'Variegata' (LEFT), shown with the original species (RIGHT).*

Fatsia japonica 'Variegata'

ARALIACEAE ▪ FALSE CASTOR OIL PLANT (OR FIGLEAF PALM)

CARE

LIGHT
Good light throughout the year. Green-leaved plants stand some shade if they have to.

TEMPERATURE
Room temperatures 50–70°F (10–21°C), avoiding higher levels. Healthiest growth at 60°F (15°C) in summer, 50°F (10°C) in winter.

WATERING
Generous during active growing season to keep compost nicely moist. Abstemiously in winter but compost should not dry right out.

FEEDING
Liquid feed fortnightly during active growth.

COMPOST
Soil-based mixture with extra fertilizer, for these are hungry plants. Move into a larger pot each spring, or top dress large plant. Clay pots are preferable, to prevent plant from toppling over.

PROPAGATION
Root 3–4 in (7.5–10 cm) long stem cuttings in spring, using shoots made at base of plant. Strip lower leaves, dip end in hormone rooting powder and insert in pot of moist peat/sand mix. Cover with a plastic bag and stand in filtered light at 60–65°F (15–18°C), and they should root within six weeks.

FATSIA JAPONICA is an exotic-looking foliage plant that has large leaves shaped like hands with seven to nine finger-like lobes, ranging in size from 6 in (15 cm) across in young plants to 1 ft (30 cm) or more in older plants. But its appearance is rather misleading, for it is a hardy shrub that grows happily in the garden, reaching over 6 ft (1.8 m) in height and bearing clusters of white flowers in late winter. Consequently it needs cooler conditions indoors than might be expected.

Often known as the Castor Oil Plant from its similarity to *Ricinus communis*, the true Castor Oil Plant which needs sub-tropical conditions to thrive, *Fatsia japonica* makes an imposing foliage plant some 4 ft (1.2 m) high indoors, and even then needs some pruning each year to keep it within bounds. Bear this in mind when buying a neat little youngster 1 ft (30 cm) across in a small pot. It will not remain like that for long!

Such a vigorous glossy-leaved evergreen is just right for some locations in the home. Where it is too large, try the form 'Variegata' instead. This is a less vigorous grower, and its white splashed leaves make it even more attractive. But it is more dependent upon good light to retain its coloration.

ABOVE RIGHT Fatsia japonica *'Variegata'*

LEFT The original Fatsia japonica.

Faucaria tigrina

AIZOACEAE ▪ TIGER JAWS

—CARE—

LIGHT
Good light and some sun throughout the year.

TEMPERATURE
Warm room temperatures (60–75°F/15–24°C) in summer; winter rest at 50°F (10°C).

WATERING
Enough to keep compost moist through season of active growth; barely enough to keep moist in winter.

FEEDING
Weak liquid feed monthly only during active growth.

COMPOST
Soil-based mixture 2 parts to 1 part of coarse sand. Use shallow container because roots are sparse.

PROPAGATION
Divide established clumps with several offsets during early summer.

FAUCARIA TIGRINA, a South African succulent plant, does mimic a tiger's jaws in the shape of its long fleshy leaves, and the hooked teeth with which they are armed. Its yellow flowers, which open in late summer, and look not unlike daisies, add to the tiger picture by their colour.

This plant grows by means of basal offsets which provide the gardener with a natural means of starting new plants. Like many succulents, this faucaria is grown primarily for its shape, which is interesting though perhaps not beautiful.

Ficus benjamina

MORACEAE ■ WEEPING FIG

— CARE —

LIGHT
Moderate, with some sun for a few hours a day. Variegated form needs more light to retain its colour.

TEMPERATURE
Normal warm room temperatures are suitable: 60–75°F (15–24°C), winter and summer, although it can be acclimatized to somewhat lower levels.

WATERING
With moderation to keep just moist; surface 1 in (2.5 cm) should dry out between waterings. Dislikes too much water.

FEEDING
Liquid feed twice monthly while in active growth.

COMPOST
Use soil-based mixture. Best when slightly underpotted, but move to a larger pot in spring when many roots grow on the surface of the compost or from the drainhole. On large plants top dress instead.

PROPAGATION
Cuttings of F. benjamina *are difficult to root. Air layering is easier although still slow.*

FICUS BENJAMINA, the Weeping Fig, is an altogether more graceful, if less impressive, plant than the popular *Ficus elastica* or rubber plant. Remember that it is by nature a tree, so it will continue to grow taller and larger until it may become too large to keep in the house any longer. It is not too rapid a grower, however, and so can be enjoyed for several seasons before it becomes an embarrassment. It is an undemanding plant amenable to quite a wide range of conditions. There is also a handsome cream-variegated form of less vigorous growth.

The plant's weeping habit is attractive, and its fresh mid-green leaves, oval with prominent points, are also pleasant. It can make a fine specimen in a tub or large pot – impressive if two or three can be grown together. While still small it could form a vertical accent to a group of lower-growing foliage plants.

A few lower leaves yellow and fall in the natural course of its life, balanced by fresh growth at the top. Scale insects may appear on its stem or twigs, giving rise to sooty mould. Keep the foliage clean by regular wiping over.

Ficus elastica

MORACEAE ▪ RUBBER PLANT

—CARE—

LIGHT
Moderate, with some sun for a few hours a day. Variegated form needs more light to retain its colour.

TEMPERATURE
Normal warm room temperatures are suitable: 60–75°F (15–24°C), winter and summer, although it can be acclimatized to somewhat lower levels.

WATERING
With moderation to keep just moist; surface 1 in (2.5 cm) should dry out between waterings. Dislikes too much water.

FEEDING
Liquid feed twice monthly while in active growth.

COMPOST
Use soil-based mixture. Best when slightly underpotted, but move to a larger pot in spring when many roots grow on the surface of the compost or from the drainhole. On large plants top dress instead.

PROPAGATION
Cuttings of F. elastica *are difficult to root. Air layering is easier although still slow.*

FICUS ELASTICA has for long been one of the most popular evergreen foliage plants for home decoration, although others now vie with it. Its glossy leaves are a magnificent rich dark green and contrast handsomely with the luxuriantly red sheath that protects the developing leaves at the top of the plant.

Generally grown as a single-stemmed specimen — a tree, in fact — this ficus can branch to form a bushier specimen. It is easy to care for but objects to either an excess or a lack of water by shedding its lower leaves. However, the yellowing and loss of one or two each season is a perfectly natural occurrence and should give no cause for anxiety.

Sponge over the plant's glossy leaves regularly to remove dust and grime. It then looks smarter and its leaves can function better.

Air layering is easier for the amateur than trying to get growth from root cuttings.

Ficus pumila

MORACEAE ▪ CREEPING FIG

—CARE—

LIGHT
Moderate, with some sun for a few hours a day. Variegated form needs more light to retain its colour.

TEMPERATURE
Normal warm room temperatures are suitable: 60–75°F (15–24°C), winter and summer, although it can be acclimatized to somewhat lower levels.

WATERING
With moderation to keep just moist; surface 1 in (2.5 cm) should dry out between waterings. Dislikes too much water.

FEEDING
Liquid feed twice monthly while in active growth.

COMPOST
Ficus pumila *and* F. sagittata *prefer a peat-based potting mixture.*

PROPAGATION
Root from 6in (15cm) tip cuttings in a peat/sand mix in the spring. If plant has layered itself, then remove rooted pieces and use.

FICUS PUMILA, sometimes called *F. repens*, the Creeping Fig, is a modest creeping foliage plant from East Asia. It is valuable for furnishing and spreading over whatever support is provided for it, such as a moss pole, and roots as it goes. It forms small heart-shaped leaves on thin wiry stems which can make a pleasant ground cover under other plants in a trough. The plant can also be grown in a hanging basket and allowed to trail downward.

Ficus sagittata, formerly *F. radicans,* is a rather similar plant, but its leaves are larger and its stems sturdier. It is generally grown as a basket plant. The form 'Variegata' which has white edges to its leaves is more eye-catching although a somewhat less vigorous grower. *F. pumila* and *F. sagittata* prefer a peat-based mixture.

To propagate, root from 6 in (15 cm) long tip cuttings in spring in peat/sand mix, or remove rooted pieces from established plants that have layered themselves.

Gasteria verrucosa

LILIACEAE ▪ WARTY GASTERIA

—CARE—

LIGHT
Moderate light, but not strong, direct sun.

TEMPERATURE
Normal warm room temperatures, 60–75°F (15–24°C) while actively growing, but about 50°F (10°C) during winter rest.

WATERING
Moderate while growing; allow to partly dry out between waterings. Keep barely moist in winter.

FEEDING
None, because it forces unnatural growth.

COMPOST
Soil-based mix 3 parts, 1 part coarse sand. Use a broad container to allow for the spread of offsets.

PROPAGATION
Pot up rooted offsets or root those without roots in summer. Allow the latter to dry for a couple of days before insertion.

GASTERIA VERRUCOSA, a South African succulent, is grown both for its distinctive clumps of fleshy leaves and for its tall stems of attractive tubular flowers, which appear in late spring and early summer. Its tapering fleshy leaves are 4–6 in (10–15 cm) long and covered in whitish warts referred to in its epithet *verrucosa*.

This plant is somewhat exceptional in that although it is a succulent it enjoys a degree of shade. In the wild it grows in the shadow of larger plants; in the home it is not so dependent on the light of a window as are other succulents.

Grevillea robusta

PROTEACEAE ▪ SILK OAK

CARE

LIGHT
Give bright light, although not fierce sun. Provide as much light as possible in winter.

TEMPERATURE
A very tolerant plant, but maintain at least 45°F (7°C) in winter. Around 60–75°F (15–24°C) in summer, provided that higher temperatures are associated with high humidity by standing the pot on moist pebbles.

WATERING
As necessary in summer to keep compost well moistened, but allow the surface to dry out between waterings. Keep barely moist in winter, with longer interval between waterings. If too dry the plant sheds its lower leaves.

FEEDING
Liquid feed monthly during the season of active growth.

COMPOST
Prefers a lime-free soil-based mixture. Move plants into larger pots in spring, perhaps again in late summer if growing strongly, to ensure they are adequately fed.

PROPAGATION
Grevilleas are normally grown from seed, and it is simplest to buy in seedlings in 2½ in (6.3 cm) pots. As an experiment try germinating some in a moist lime-free seed-sowing mix at about 60°F (15°C) in soft light. This is best done in a propagating-case or on a well-lit but not hot windowsill. Seedlings reach 1½ in (3.8 cm) high, large enough to pot into separate pots, within six weeks or so.

GREVILLEA ROBUSTA, the Australian silk oak, makes a noble forest tree more than 100 ft (30 m) high in a suitable environment. Indoors it makes a pleasant ferny-leaved evergreen foliage plant that looks particularly attractive in contrast to other foliage and flowering plants. A quick grower, it most often has to be discarded and replaced after two seasons, because it becomes too tall (and possibly also bare at the base).

Its compound leaves can be 12–15 in long and divided into many feathery leaflets; they are silky on the back, hence the name silk oak. This tree does not flower indoors because no house is large enough for it to be able to do so.

Gynura sarmentosa

COMPOSITAE ▪ PURPLE PASSION VINE

— CARE —

LIGHT
Good light, with some sunshine.

TEMPERATURE
Normal warm temperatures, 60–75°F (15–24°C), with a minimum of 55°F (13°C).

WATERING
Moderate in summer to keep compost moist, a minimum in winter so that it is barely moist. Keep water off hairy leaves, where droplets could cause marking in bright light.

FEEDING
Liquid feed fortnightly once a month all the year round to help but not force growth.

COMPOST
Use soil-based mixture. Move plants into larger pots as necessary, but replace every two years.

PROPAGATION
Root 3–4 in (7.5–10 cm) tip cuttings in moist peat/sand mix in spring. They should root within three weeks in moderate light and 70°F (21°C).

GYNURA SARMENTOSA is a trailing plant of the daisy family, treasured for its foliage, which is covered with rich purple hairs. It is a most handsome plant while young but tends to become straggly with age. For this reason, prune back its growths to keep it compact, and replace with a new plant from a cutting every second year.

This gynura produces tiny orange daisy flowers in spring, but they are not showy enough to be worth keeping; they also smell unpleasant, and so are best removed.

Although an exotic from Indonesia, this is a comparatively undemanding plant the colouration of which can make a striking contrast with that of other foliage plants, not least those with cream and green variegation.

Haworthia margaritifera

LILIACEAE ▪ PEARL PLANT

—CARE—

LIGHT
Good light, but not direct sun.

TEMPERATURE
Warm room temperatures in summer 60–75°F/15–24°F); cooler in winter when resting from late autumn to early spring – below 58°F (14°C), although the plant can tolerate 40°F (4°C).

WATERING
Moderate during summer, allow to dry out between waterings. Keep barely moist in winter.

FEEDING
None required.

COMPOST
Soil-based mixture with extra part of coarse sand.

PROPAGATION
Remove offsets in summer. If not already rooted, leave to dry for three days before setting in compost.

HAWORTHIA MARGARITIFERA is a spiky-leaved South African succulent plant often grown on sunny windowsills, where its drought-resistance is a great advantage. It is quick to form offsets around the main leaf rosette, and these provide a ready means of producing new plants.

Not unlike a spikier version of the houseleek (sempervivum), this haworthia is distinguished by the warty white markings on its leaves, from which it was called the pearl plant. When the rosette is mature enough, tiny tubular white flowers form on a tall wiry stem, but they are so insignificant as to be best cut off.

Hedera canariensis 'Variegata'

ARALIACEAE ▪ CANARY ISLAND IVY

—CARE—

LIGHT
Good light; some sunshine essential.

TEMPERATURE
Very tolerant, but it needs extra humidity at higher temperatures. Mist over frequently – red spider mite can be troublesome in a hot, dry atmosphere. Keep cool (50°F (10°C) in winter while light is poor to avoid forcing growth.

WATERING
Enough to keep compost quite moist while actively growing; less in winter while resting.

FEEDING
Liquid feed twice a month while actively growing.

COMPOST
Prefers soil-based compost mixture. Move into larger pot in spring each year if root development shows it necessary. Could set several plants round the rim of a larger pot, or in a hanging basket.

PROPAGATION
Ivies naturally form aerial roots, and so are simple to root either in water or in damp peat/sand mixture. Root several 3 in (7.5 cm) cuttings round rim of small 3 in (7.5 cm) pot, then pot on into larger size when rooted to make bold display. Cover cuttings with polythene bag and keep warm and well lit until rooted after about a month.

HEDERA CANARIENSIS 'Variegata', although closely related to common (English) ivy, has larger leaves and generally rather softer growth. Once acclimatized to the outdoors, however, it is reasonably hardy. Often known as 'Gloire de Marengo', this variegated form is a handsome plant suitable for training in various ways – over a few canes or an extensive trellis, for instance. Given encouragement, it can be quite a vigorous growing plant.

Its leaf stalks are deep red and its leaves grey-green and cream. The amount of variegation varies considerably from leaf to leaf, some being almost entirely cream.

Hedera helix 'Glacier'

ARALIACEAE ▪ ENGLISH IVY

— CARE —

LIGHT
Good light; some sunshine essential.

TEMPERATURE
Very tolerant, but it needs extra humidity at higher temperatures. Mist over frequently – red spider mite can be troublesome in a hot, dry atmosphere. Keep cool (50°F (10°C) in winter while light is poor to avoid forcing growth.

WATERING
Enough to keep compost quite moist while actively growing; less in winter while resting.

FEEDING
Liquid feed twice a month while actively growing.

COMPOST
Prefers soil-based compost mixture. Move into larger pot in spring each year if root development shows it necessary. Could set several plants round the rim of a larger pot, or in a hanging basket.

PROPAGATION
Ivies naturally form aerial roots, and so are simple to root either in water or in damp peat/sand mixture. Root several 3 in (7.5 cm) cuttings round rim of small 3 in (7.5 cm) pot, then pot on into larger size when rooted to make bold display. Cover cuttings with polythene bag and keep warm and well lit until rooted after about a month.

HEDERA HELIX, the English ivy, has contributed a range of different selected forms, varying from the original in leaf colour or shape, to the modern assortment of house plants. They have the great advantages that they are neat and cheerful and easy to please, and can be increased without much effort.

'Glacier' has typical ivy leaves 1 in (2.5 cm) across, pleasantly variegated mid-green and grey-green with white splashes and pink edges. Less vigorous than the original species, it is nonetheless quite a robust grower and should have the tips of its growth pinched out occasionally to keep it bushy and within bounds.

The main cultural requirement of variegated ivies is good light. In shade they lose their attractive colouring and grow loose and weaker. They make ideal basket plants – especially when several varieties with contrasting leaf colouring are put together. Their trailing or cascading habit makes them valuable for contrast in groups of foliage plants. They make fine individual specimens in pots too, although the effect is less exciting than when grouped.

Heliotropium peruvianum

BORAGINACEAE ▪ HELIOTROPE

— CARE —

LIGHT
Good light, though not fierce sun.

TEMPERATURE
Normal room temperatures: 60–70°F (15–21°C) in summer; 40–55°F (4–13°C) in winter.

WATERING
Moderate to keep moist in summer; more abstemious in winter.

FEEDING
Liquid feed fortnightly during active growth.

COMPOST
Soil-based mixture. Move into larger pots in spring as necessary.

PROPAGATION
Root 3 in (7.5 cm) stem cuttings in summer in moist peat/sand mix in 70°F (21°C). Or sow seeds in spring.

Heliotropum peruvianum *'Marine', a variety with flowers of a deeper colour.*

HELIOTROPIUM PERVIANUM is valued on two scores – for its purple flowers, which can range from pale lavender to an almost black-purple; and for its sweet, rich, scent, reminiscent of cherry pie, as its popular name points out.

By nature a shrubby plant that becomes woody at the base, it can be kept for some years or trained as a standard plant on a long leg. But because flowering tends to deteriorate with age, it pays to start with new plants each year, bought in or raised from cuttings. Watch out for pests, particularly whitefly which love it.

It is best treated as a valuable temporary plant, to add colour and scent to room decoration.

Helxine soleirolii

URTICACEAE ▪ BABY'S TEARS (OR MIND-YOUR-OWN-BUSINESS)

—CARE—

LIGHT
Enjoys good light, provided that it is not scorching. Adapts to moderate shade.

TEMPERATURE
Normal room temperatures: 50–75°F (10–24°C); a minimum of 45°F (7°C) in winter.

WATERING
Keep compost moist always. Plant's fleshy growth soon collapses if it dries out.

FEEDING
Weak liquid feed fortnightly in season of active growth.

COMPOST
Soil-based mixture with extra one-third peat.

PROPAGATION
By division during active season. Small rooted pieces quickly establish in small pots of moist compost.

HELXINE SOLEIROLII, recently renamed *Soleirolia soleirolii*, is a humble creeping plant incidentally related to the stinging nettle, and is a native of Corsica. But it is a strong grower which, as its familiar name 'Mind-Your-Own-Business' implies, is likely to spread where it is not wanted if it gets the chance.

Grown in individual small pots (3–4 in/7.5–10 cm) it forms pleasant hummocks of fresh green foliage sometimes mistakenly referred to as moss. There is also a cheerful gold-leaved form, which looks just like sunshine if it gets enough light.

Helxine can form a pleasant-looking carpet under other plants, but this should only be attempted where it can be kept firmly under control or where its wandering habits are acceptable. The plant's main demands are for moist soil and humid air.

Heptapleurum arboricola

ARALIACEAE ▪ PARASOL PLANT

—CARE—

LIGHT
Good light, but not full sun.

TEMPERATURE
Warm room temperatures: 60–75°F (15–24°C); a minimum of 60°F (15°C) in winter.

WATERING
Moderate, so that compost is moist but not wet.

FEEDING
Liquid feed fortnightly during season of active growth.

COMPOST
Soil-based compost, with extra one-third peat if watering is likely to compact it overmuch.

PROPAGATION
Root 3–4 in (7.5–10 cm) long tip cuttings in spring. Trim beneath a leaf joint, dip in hormone rooting powder, and insert in pot of peat/sand mixture. Cover with a plastic bag. Temperature of 65–75°F (18–24°C) essential to success.

HEPTAPLEURUM ARBORICOLA is a handsome evergreen the radiating leaflets of which have earned it its familiar name of Parasol Plant. Left to its own devices it rapidly grows into a tree-like specimen – but fortunately it is amenable to training. If its top is pinched out it then forms a pleasing bushy plant, more suitable for indoor decoration. It is related to Schefflera and is sometimes sold under this name.

It is an easily managed plant provided that it gets good light and warmth and a humid atmosphere, and that its glossy leaves are wiped clear of dust from time to time.

Hibiscus rosa-sinensis

MALVACEAE ▪ ROSE OF CHINA

— CARE —

LIGHT
Plenty of good light, though not fierce summer sun.

TEMPERATURE
Normal warm room temperatures: 60–75°F (15–24°C); a winter minimum of 55°F (13°C).

WATERING
Keep moist always to support strong growth – daily for much of the summer, less in cooler, shadier conditions. Spray foliage with water occasionally on warm days.

FEEDING
Give high potash feed twice monthly while in active growth.

COMPOST
Soil-based mixture, with little extra peat if necessary to prevent compaction after regular watering. Move plant into larger pot each year, or top dress larger plants.

PROPAGATION
Root 3–4 in (7.5–10 cm) long stem tip cuttings in spring or summer in peat/sand mixture; cover with a plastic bag. They should root within a month, when the bag can be removed and the plant allowed to establish before being potted in larger pots of soil-based mixture.

HIBISCUS ROSA-SINENSIS is by nature a strong-growing sub-tropical shrub, and is widely planted as a decorative garden plant in warmer parts of the world, where it forms a magnificent display of large trumpet flowers. In the home it grows less strongly, but it may still prove necessary to prune its growths back quite severely in early spring to ensure a neat, compact plant later in the season.

Good light is essential with this plant, as is sufficient but not excessive moisture; otherwise it is not difficult to manage. On the credit side, its exotic blooms are worth any effort taken to produce them.

Hippeastrum Hybrid

AMARYLLIDACEAE ▪ AMARYLLIS

CARE

LIGHT

Give good light and some sun while in active growth. It is affected by light while dormant. Expose to sun after flowring until dormancy in order to build up bulb for next flowering.

TEMPERATURE

Normal warm room temperatures: 60–65°F (15–18°C). Higher temperatures shorten the life of bloom – normally a week or so, with plant decorative for a fortnight.

WATERING

Moderate throughout the active growth period, with restraint until newly potted bulb is well rooted and again in autumn to encourage onset of leaf loss and dormancy. Keep dry throughout winter until flower bud or first leaf shows above neck of bulb.

FEEDING

Normal liquid feed twice a month from completion of flowering to midsummer, then high potash feed until autumn only.

COMPOST

Use soil-based compost mix provide adequate drainage by means of a layer of shords in bottom of pot. Only half-bury bulb, leaving the 'shoulders' above the surface, and make firm. Replace some of the tired compost with fresh each spring after flowering, but disturb bulb as little as possible.

PROPAGATION

Remove any offsets that have formed beside parent bulb and pot separately. Raising from seed involved several years' wait for flowers and the coloration is unreliable, so this is not recommended for the home gardener.

HIPPEASTRUMS, from Tropical America, are among the most striking of all bulb flowers and not difficult to grow indoors. They are widely sold under the name Amaryllis, although the technical name *Amaryllis belladonna* is that of the Belladonna Lily, a different hardy bulb from South Africa.

They are usually bought as dry bulbs, potted, and then flowered in late winter or early spring, after which the strap-shaped foliage develops. They have a distinct dormant season in autumn and early winter, when the foliage dies off, before the cycle begins again.

Bulbs are sold specially prepared to flower in time for Christmas or New Year, but these revert to normal flowering time in subsequent years. The large trumpet flowers can be 6 in (15 cm) across, three or four to a stem; the stem can rise 15–18 in (33.8–45 cm) above the bulb. Two stems arise from the largest bulbs. Colour can range from scarlet, pink or white to blooms streaked or flared in two colours, or with distinctly coloured borders.

Although easy to bring flower on a bulb prepared by a nursery, more skill is required to persuade the Amaryllis to flower again the next season. It is vital to feed and water the bulb after flowering in order to recharge its energies.

Hoya carnosa

ASCLEPIADACEAE ▪ HONEY PLANT, WAX PLANT (OR PORCELAIN FLOWER)

—CARE—

LIGHT
Good light, with several hours of sun per day.

TEMPERATURE
Normal room temperatures of 50–70°F (10–21°C) suit hoyas.

WATERING
Moderate, to keep compost moist while in growth. Only enough to keep slightly moist while resting.

FEEDING
Give high potash feed fortnightly only while in active growth.

COMPOST
Soil-based mixture preferred. Move plants into larger pots annually in spring if necessary, or top dress with fresh compost.

SEASONAL CARE
Do not remove faded flower clusters in usual way because spurs produce more flowers later. Cut off only individual spent flowers. Stem cuttings 3–4 in (7.5–10 cm) long can be rooted in moist peat/sand mixture in spring. Strip away lower leaves, dip end in hormone rooting powder, insert, then cover with a plastic bag. Keep warm (65–70°F/18–21°C) in filtered light. Should root within two months.

HOYA CARNOSA is an easily-grown climbing plant from South-Eastern Asia and the subtropical northern parts of Australia, valued for its clusters of long-lasting sweet-scented flowers, which appear from late spring to early autumn.

This plant can, where there is space enough, be trained over an indoor trellis. Alternatively, grow it in a large pot (8 in/20 cm), training it around a ring of wire so it takes up less room. This also concentrates its flowers for a more intense effect.

Each tiny bloom, about ½ in (1.3 cm) across, is white or very pale pink with a red centre. They are borne in clusters of 15 to 20, and last for many weeks. The scent is sweet and rich.

BELOW *The perfumed flowers of the dwarf species,* Hoya bella.

Hypoestes phyllostachya

ACANTHACEAE ▪ FRECKLE FACE (OR POLKA DOT PLANT)

— CARE —

LIGHT
Bright but filtered light to ensure good leaf colour.

TEMPERATURE
Normal warm room temperatures, 60–75°F (15–24°C; a minimum of 59°F (14°C).

WATERING
Moderate to keep compost moist in active season; less in semi-dormant winter season.

FEEDING
Liquid feed fortnightly while in active growth.

COMPOST
Soil-based mixture. Move plants into larger pots in spring if present pots filled with roots. Keep plants compact at about 1 ft (30 cm) high by pruning. Replace tired-looking plants.

PROPAGATION
From seeds in spring or 3–4 in (7.5–10 cm) stem cuttings in moist peat/sand mix covered with a plastic bag.

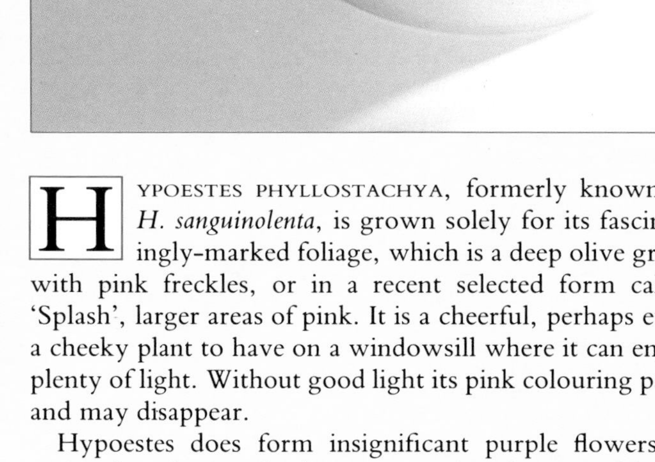

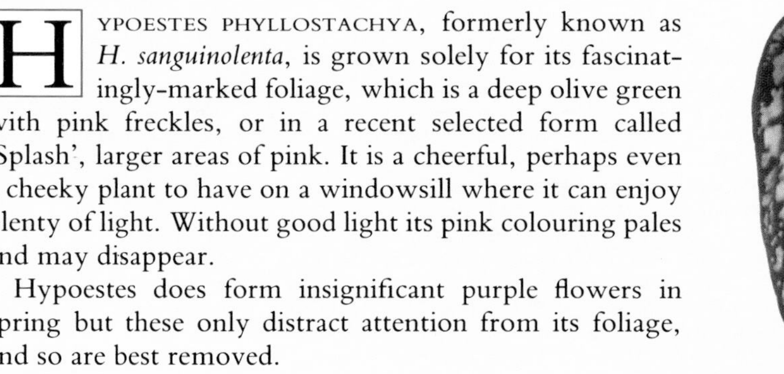

HYPOESTES PHYLLOSTACHYA, formerly known as *H. sanguinolenta*, is grown solely for its fascinatingly-marked foliage, which is a deep olive green with pink freckles, or in a recent selected form called 'Splash', larger areas of pink. It is a cheerful, perhaps even a cheeky plant to have on a windowsill where it can enjoy plenty of light. Without good light its pink colouring pales and may disappear.

Hypoestes does form insignificant purple flowers in spring but these only distract attention from its foliage, and so are best removed.

Jasminum polyanthum

OLEACEAE ▪ PINK JASMINE

—CARE—

LIGHT
Give bright light, including some sun.

TEMPERATURE
Keep cool in summer – no higher than 60°F (15°C), nor lower than 45°F (7°C).

WATERING
Give plenty of water while in growth so compost is always moist. Semi-dormant in winter, it must then be kept drier, although never parched.

FEEDING
Liquid feed twice a month while in active growth.

COMPOST
Use soil-based compost. Move plants into larger pots in early summer, or top dress if already in a large pot.

PROPAGATION
Root some stem cuttings (2½ in/6.3 cm) tips trimmed beneath a leaf joint (or short side shoots removed with a 'heel' of older wood) in late summer in a moist peat/sand mixture. Cover with a plastic bag and stand in filtered light. They should root in about a month.

JASMINUM POLYANTHUM is a strong-growing climber cultivated for its white flowers, flushed pink on the outside and sweetly scented. These appear early in the year, from late winter to early or mid spring. It is widely sold by florists just as it is coming into flower.

Its early flowering season and gorgeous, unforgettable scent are its two main recommendations. On the other hand, it does demand good light in which to thrive, and is a very vigorous plant that takes some handling after it has flowered. It needs severe pruning then, and fresh compost and good light if it is to flower in its second season. It is not hardy enough to plant out in the garden.

Kalanchoe blossfeldiana

CRASSULACEAE ▪ FLAMING KATY

—CARE—

LIGHT
Give plenty of light on a sunny windowsill.

TEMPERATURE
It is happy at summer room temperatures, 60–75°F (15–24°C). Best discarded before winter.

WATERING
Water with restraint or the leaves become flabby and flowering is reduced.

FEEDING
Liquid feed once or twice a month while blooming.

COMPOST
Use soil-based mixture with more coarse sand or perlite added. Also generous layer of clay shards in the bottom of the pot for efficient drainage.

PROPAGATION
Tip cuttings can be rooted in spring, but are so difficult to bring to flower that it is best to buy plants in bud.

KALANCHOE BLOSSFELDIANA is a decorative succulent plant grown mostly for its brightly-coloured long-lasting flowers, which usually are a brilliant scarlet although there are magenta-pink, yellow and orange forms. As a succulent, it does not demand as much water as most flowering plants, nor as frequent watering, but never allow it to become parched.

This plant's fleshy rich green leaves form a fine background for its scarlet (or other-coloured) flowers, but although acceptable are not sufficiently interesting to make a non-flowering plant worth having. Consequently, because it is difficult to get a kalanchoe to flower again in normal home conditions, it is best to discard it after its two- or three-month season of glory, and to start afresh the following year.

The original *K. blossfeldiana* was a tall and rather lanky plant, but those now sold are far more compact, averaging 12 in (30 cm) tall, with miniatures like 'Vulcan' as little as 6 in (15 cm) high.

Kalanchoe daigremontiana

CRASSULACEAE ▪ DEVIL'S BACKBONE (OR MOTHER OF THOUSANDS)

—CARE—

LIGHT
Likes good light but not fierce sunshine.

TEMPERATURE
Enjoys typical room temperatures of 60–75°F (15–24°C) winter and summer, although it survives lower temperatures if kept on the dry side.

WATERING
Adapted to a highly seasonal rainfall, so water moderately from spring to early autumn, very sparingly in winter.

FEEDING
Liquid feed monthly during active growth.

COMPOST
Best in a soil-based mixture, perhaps with extra sand added for better drainage. Pot into a larger pot in spring when necessary. Replace plant with a young one when it gets too large and lanky.

PROPAGATION
Plantlets provide for easy propagation. Transplant some already rooted in plant's pot, or pick some off leaves and set in potting compost. They root quickly and develop within 2–4 weeks.

KALANCHOE DAIGREMONTIANA, a succulent plant from Madagascar, formerly known as *Bryophyllum diagremontianum*, makes a fascinating windowsill plant. The many tiny plantlets that form on its leaf margins are its most prominent feature and provide a very ready means of making more plants.

This kalanchoe grows on a single tall stem 2–3 ft (60–90 cm) tall, with opposite pairs of fleshy tooth-edged leaves and tiny plantlets between the teeth, often with the beginnings of roots visible. The plant may flower at the top, but the dull pink blooms are tiny and not very interesting.

Laurus nobilis

LAURACEAE ▪ LAUREL OR BAY TREE (OR SWEET BAY)

—*CARE*—

LIGHT
Give bright light, even direct sunlight: it is perfectly tough and hardy.

TEMPERATURE
It is happy within the range 45–75°F (7–24°C), provided that water is plentiful at high temperatures, sparse at lower ones. Keep frost-free or the roots could be damaged or leaf edges browned.

WATERING
Moderate from spring to early autumn, for it must never dry out, yet not too wet. Drier in winter, because cold wet soil can kill it.

FEEDING
Liquid feed monthly during season of active growth.

COMPOST
Soil-based mixture with extra peat added.

SEASONAL CARE
Give it an outdoor holiday in summer. Repot in spring when pot is filled with roots. Root stem cuttings in spring or late summer.

LAURUS NOBILIS, the bay tree, is a hardy evergreen bush or small tree often planted as a formal clipped specimen in a patio tub. But it can be used indoors in a similar way as a shapely foliage plant. It has the advantage of being content with cool temperatures and less frequent watering than many of the more exotic foliage plants.

It naturally forms a spreading bush shape, so it is necessary to trim it lightly with secateurs to create and maintain a more formal shape, usually that of a cone. A ball-shaped head on a clear stem, as often favoured outdoors, may not look right in the home.

Liriope muscari

LILIACEAE ▪ BIG BLUE LILY TURF

—CARE—

LIGHT
Good light, particularly for 'Variegata'.

TEMPERATURE
It is happy in a temperate room, 55–70°F (13–21°C), but tolerates heat up to 85°F (30°C).

WATERING
Moderate to keep compost nicely moist while growing. Just enough to keep from parching during semi-dormant season.

FEEDING
Liquid feed fortnightly while growth is active.

COMPOST
Soil-based mixture. Move plant into larger pot in spring only when it has filled its present pot.

PROPAGATION
By splitting an established clump of growth into pieces with ten or a dozen leaves each.

LIRIOPE MUSCARI is a hardy garden plant that was introduced from China and Japan purely for the sake of its spikes of purple-blue flowers (which do, as its name clearly indicates, resemble those of the grape hyacinth or muscari).

This plant grows 12–15 in (30–38 cm) high and has a cluster of straplike leaves springing from soil level. The flowers develop in late summer and contrast well with the foliage. However, even more decorative is the form 'Variegata', of which the leaves are striped yellow along their length, a particularly cheerful combination of colours. Like all variegated plants it demands good light to display its full colouring.

Lithops fulleri

AIZOACEAE ▪ LIVING STONES

— CARE —

LIGHT
Good light with several hours of direct sun each day all year are essential for good health.

TEMPERATURE
It is happy in normal room temperatures – 60–75°F (15–24°C) in summer, 50–65°F (10–18°C) in winter; 50°F (10°C) is the safe minimum.

WATERING
Give a minimum to keep the compost moist, allowing it to almost dry out between waterings, from spring to autumn. During the long winter rest period give none; they subsist on water stored in their leaves.

FEEDING
So sparse is their diet in the desert that they need no feeding from us.

COMPOST
Use equal parts of soil-based compost and sharp sand with a generous layer of broken clay shards in the base of the container to provide sharp drainage. Although small, lithops need normal-depth pots to accommodate their tap roots.

SEASONAL CARE
Clumps of 'stones' may need dividing every three or four years. Do this in early summer, giving new plants filtered light and little water until established.

Lithops can be raised from seeds in spring but take several years to reach mature size. Add extra sand to the sowing mixture and provide a good drainage layer of shingle to carry away excess water.

LITHOPS FULLERI is one of several species of succulent plant that eke out an existence in the deserts of Southern Africa and mimic the pebbles around them to avoid being browsed by passing animals.

Their appeal as house-plants is limited; they are small – little more than 1 in (2.5 cm) across – and not especially showy. But they are intriguing and require the minimum of care, and so could appeal to a busy flat-dweller who has a windowsill sunny enough to keep them happy.

The 'stones' of *L. fulleri* consist of a pair of fleshy leaves with a ¼ in (0.6 cm) deep slit between them. Grey in colour, their upper surfaces are patterned with brown lines. Small 1 in (2.5 cm) white flowers open from the slit in autumn. The 'stone' grows on a short stem beneath the soil from a longish taproot. After flowering, the leaves wither, to be followed by new ones. The plants develop into clumps, but progress is slow.

Maranta leuconeura kerchoveana

MARANTACEAE ▪ PRAYER PLANT (OR RABBIT TRACKS)

—CARE—

LIGHT
Moderate light; strong sun fades leaf colouring and can scorch tender leaves.

TEMPERATURE
Warm room temperatures all year, 65–75°F (18–24°C); a minimum of 55°F (13°C). Provide extra humidity at higher temperatures by standing the pot on a tray of moist pebbles.

FEEDING
Liquid feed fortnightly while actively growing.

COMPOST
Soil-based with a little extra peat to keep mixture porous. Use shallow containers because roots do not run deep.

PROPAGATION
Divide established clumps in spring, or root stem cuttings during summer. Cuttings should be 3–4 in (7.5–10 cm) long with three or four leaves. Remove lower leaves; trim beneath a leaf joint, dip in hormone rooting powder, and inset in moist peat/sand mix. Cover with a plastic bag or put in a warm propagator. Should root in six weeks. Repot in potting compost when well rooted.

MARANTA LEUCONEURA KERCHOVEANA has for long been a favourite foliage house-plant because it is compact, attractive to look at, and easy to manage – although it cannot withstand neglect. Its leaves fold together at night, earning it its familiar name of prayer plant. The original species has green leaves with white nerves or veins, as the name *leuconeura* indicates; but the form *kerchoveana* has dark brown markings between the veins which have been likened to rabbit's tracks, hence its other name.

Another jungle plant from South America, this maranta revels in warmth and high humidity, although it is more tolerant than others of its family. *M. leuconeura erythroneura* is a more highly decorative form that has red leaf veins and purplish red undersides to its dark and light green leaves, but it must have tropical conditions or else it pines away and dies.

Monstera deliciosa

ARACEAE ▪ SWISS CHEESE PLANT (OR SPLITLEAF PHILODENDRON)

— CARE —

LIGHT
Good but filtered light in summer. Best possible light in winter or could become drawn and weak.

TEMPERATURE
Warm room temperature, 60–75°F (15–24°C) all year, although it can withstand a somewhat lower figure. Ensure adequate humidity at high temperatures.

WATERING
Just enough to keep compost barely moist; allow the surface to dry out between waterings.

FEEDING
Liquid feed twice a month while in active growth.

COMPOST
Use soil-based mixture (3 parts) with extra 1 part of coarse peat. Move plant into larger pot each spring until largest size is reached, then top dress instead.

PROPAGATION
Root a tip cutting in peat/ sand mixture in spring, covering the pot with a plastic bag to keep in humidity and standing it in filtered light in warmth. Or air layer plant

MONSTERA DELICIOSA is one of the most widely grown of all foliage house plants; it is tough and good tempered, handsome and long-lived. By nature it is a thick-stemmed climbing plant, so some support is essential. A moss pole (a plastic mesh cylinder filled with sphagnum moss) suits it well: it can root into the damp moss, which imitates the moss-covered bark of some tropical tree. Train its aerial roots into the moss pole or into compost in a pot.

The intriguing large perforations in its leaves are intended to allow storm winds to pass through rather than tear them to shreds. These are one of its main attractions as a decorative plant. Regularly clean dust off the leaves with a damp cloth. Note that leaves of young half-developed plants do not show these holes. Just be patient – they will appear when the plants mature.

These easily-managed plants are vigorous growers and need plenty of room. A variegated form with white-splashed leaves is even more handsome, and not such a strong grower. In high temperatures and humidity (to a degree unlikely in the home), monsteras form white arum flowers, followed by edible white fruits.

BELOW The deeply serrated leaves benefit from occasional cleaning with a damp cloth, but do not clean young, soft leaves as they are easily damaged.

Neoregelia carolinae 'Tricolor'

BROMELIACEAE ▪ BLUSHING BROMELIAD

—CARE—

LIGHT
Good light, with some sun.

TEMPERATURE
Warm room temperatures, 60–75°F (15–24°C); a minimum of 50°F (10°C).

WATERING
Keep compost just moist by moderate watering. Fill centre of rosette with soft water and replace with fresh monthly to keep it healthy.

FEEDING
Give weak liquid feed fortnightly in active season, to 'vase' as well as compost.

COMPOST
Light mixture of 2 parts coarse peat and 1 part coarse sand. Move to larger pot only when necessary.

PROPAGATION
Root young rosettes, or carefully transplant any that have already rooted, into 3 in (7.5 cm) pots of peat/sand mixture in spring.

NEOREGELIA CAROLINAE 'Tricolor' is one of the most highly decorative of the bromeliads (pineapple family). Its main attraction lies in the rich beetroot-red colour in the centre of its leaf rosette, which develops as it approaches flowering time. The centre of the rosette forms a typical bromeliad 'vase', which needs to be kept filled with (soft) water. Tiny, insignificant flowers form in the vase, untroubled by the wet conditions.

The form 'Tricolor' that is generally offered for sale is also marked with longitudinal yellow stripes on its leaves which form a striking contrast to the reddish heart of the plant. It is about 18 in (45 cm) across and up to 9 in (23 cm) high. Remember that bromeliad rosettes die after flowering, so consider rooting one of the young rosettes which form to replace it.

Nephrolepis exaltata

POLYPODIACEAE ▪ SWORD FERN

—CARE—

LIGHT
Good light, but not bright sun. Tolerates slight shade.

TEMPERATURE
Normal warm room temperatures, 60–75°F (15–24°C); a winter minimum of 50°F (10°C).

WATERING
Give plenty of water to keep compost moist all the time, unless temperature falls below 55°F (13°C), when compost should be kept only just moist.

FEEDING
Liquid feed ferns in soil-based compost monthly, those in peat-based compost twice as often.

COMPOST
Either equal-parts soil-based compost and peat, or peat-based mixture. Move plant into larger pot in spring as necessary, or tease out some of old, exhausted compost and replace with fresh.

PROPAGATION
From plantlets formed on runners, which are potted in 3 in (7.5 cm) pots and severed from the parent when rooted.

NEPHROLEPIS EXALTATA is a vigorous grower that produces a cluster of fronds some 2–3 ft (60–90 cm) long, each divided into many pinnae ('feathers'). It can develop into a most handsome foliage plant, and has the advantage over many house plants that it grows happily in slight shade, although it prefers good light for the best results.

This fern grows from a rhizome (horizontal stem on the surface of the soil) from which it sends out wiry runners with plantlets at the ends. These can be encouraged to root into the pot to extend the size of the plant, or be rooted in separate small pots as a means of propagating new plants.

RIGHT Microcoelum weddellianum; *the narrow leaflets give this palm its special appeal.*

Palm Trees

PALMACEAE

Palm Trees

PALMACEAE

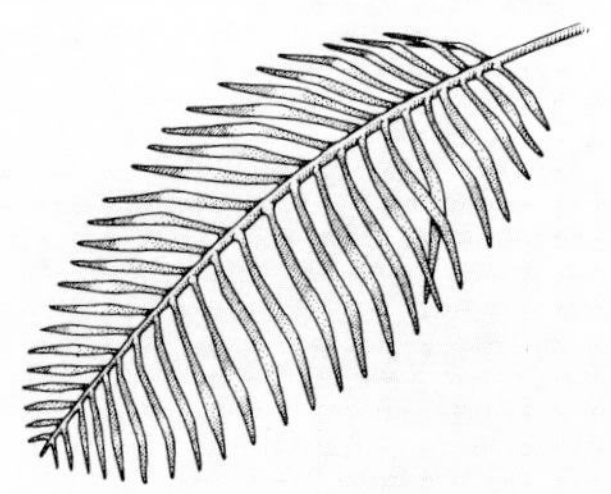

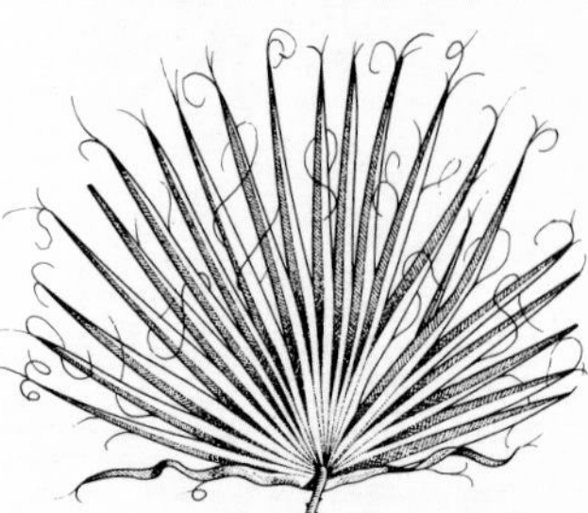

Palms fall into two divisions: those with feathery – 'pinnate' – fronds (top) and those with fan-like – 'palmate' – ones (above).

ABOVE Howea forsteriana.

RIGHT Phoenix canariensis.

If you want your house-plants few, large and imposing to give your room character, or if you are after a Palm Court atmosphere or a whiff of the South Seas, a palm tree in a tub or large ornamental pot could certainly oblige. Given reasonable light and warmth and moderate watering, a palm is little trouble – until it becomes too large for the space available. Even this can be catered for by the so-called Parlour Palm (see *Chamaedorea elegans*, often sold as *Neanthe bella*).

The real Palm Court palm is *Howea forsteriana,* the Paradise Palm, once commonly known as a Kentia. This is a stronger-growing plant than *Chamaedorea,* forming a small tree in a few years, with arching stems 2½–3 ft (0.8–0.9 m) long, bearing many leaflets held out horizontally. It can easily extend 4–5 ft (1.2–1.5 m) high and 6 ft (1.8 m) across, so be careful to allow space for this when planning your room decoration.

Palm Trees

PALMACEAE

—CARE—

LIGHT
Good but filtered light. Palms can stand some shade but in poor light may become drawn and weak.

TEMPERATURE
Tolerant, but prefer 65–75°F (18–24°C) in summer; lower in winter – 55°F (13°C) minimum. Keep the surrounding air humid by misting and standing the container on a tray of moist pebbles. Leaf tips could brown if air is too dry, and red spider mites could appear.

WATERING
Plenty during active growing season, but with good drainage. Less in winter so that compost is only just moist.

FEEDING
Give weak liquid feed monthly during active growth only.

COMPOST
Soil-based mixture 3 parts with extra 1 part of peat to improve porosity. Only move palm into larger pot wher obviously necessary. Firm gently because the roots are brittle.

SEASONAL CARE
Mist foliage regularly when air is dry to discourage red spider mites. If present, these turn leaflets yellow and mottled. Also watch for scale insects along stems.
Palms cannot be propagated in home conditions.

Palm Trees

PALMACEAE

Microcoelum weddellianum, the Weddell Palm from Brazil, often offered as *Cocos* or *Syagrus weddelliana*, is less vigorous than the howea, although it does grow to tree-like proportions after some years. Its special beauty is in its considerably narrower pinnae (leaflets) which give it a much daintier look.

Growing indoors perhaps 3 ft (90 cm) high and 2 ft (60 cm) wide, with fronds 2 ft 6 in to 3 ft (75–90 cm) long, a microcoelum is certainly easier to accommodate than a howea, and its light, airy texture may fit better with modern furnishings.

Chamaerops humilis, the European Fan Palm, is quite distinct from the other palms described here. Its fronds are arranged palmately (like the fingers of a hand) on stems some 15 in (37.5 cm) long. It is a handsome and exotic-looking palm, growing about 4 – 5 ft (1.2–1.5 m) high, but due care should be taken of the teeth on its leaf stalks, which deserve respect.

Phoenix canariensis, the Canary Island Date Palm, makes a fine tub plant. Whereas it is possible to raise a date palm from a stone, that would result in *P. dactylifera,* a quicker-growing and larger tree that is also less attractive than its Canary Island cousin. So if you fancy a palm in a large container in your room, consider *P. canariensis,* with its shuttlecock of rich green fronds branching from a scaly basal stem. In a tub it makes a 6 ft (1.8 m) tall tree after some years.

Where something smaller is essential because of space, try *P. roebelinii,* which comes from South-Eastern Asia. Its fronds arch more gracefully than do those of *P. canariensis,* and its leaflets are narrower and daintier. This palm makes a 3 ft (90 cm) tall specimen, although it can spread a little wider than this.

Palm Trees

PALMACEAE

FAR LEFT Howea belmoreana, *commonly known as the Kentia palm.*

LEFT Phoenix canariensis.

ABOVE Phoenix roebelinii.

RIGHT *Mature* Chamaerops humilis *grown under glass.*

Pelargonium Species

GERANIACEAE

ABOVE *Pelargoniums look particularly good if several of the many different varieties are grown together.*

BELOW Pelargonium graveolens.

PELARGONIUM GRAVEOLENS is one of a number of species of pelargonium grown for their scented foliage. This particular kind is scented of roses, but others offer peppermint, lemon or apple scent. This group of pelargoniums generally produces small, unremarkable flowers, but *P. graveolens*' rose-pink flowers with tiny purple spots on them are well worth looking at.

This is a vigorous plant that can grow up to 3 ft (90 cm) high, although it responds well to pruning when necessary. Its leaves are deeply segmented and quite ornamental. Stem cuttings root readily.

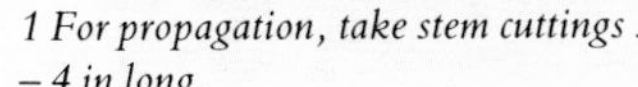

1 For propagation, take stem cuttings 3 – 4 in long.

2 Trim just under a leaf joint and dip in hormone rooting powder.

3 Most pelargonium cuttings like a peat/sand mixture; (see care chart).

PELARGONIUM HORTORUM is the name given to the many ornamental hybrids of the zonal pelargonium now far removed from any naturally-occurring species. Originating in South Africa, these somewhat succulent, drought-resistant plants are distinguished by the darker semi-circular zone in their leaves. This can be dark maroon or black. Their clusters of flowers can range from scarlet to pink, white and orange and magenta; their leaves from plain green to golden yellow or multicoloured.

They are surely the best-tempered of all indoor flowering plants, although they insist on really good light to thrive and flower well, and hate to be overwatered, which soon causes their stems to turn black and rot.

Given suitable conditions they can flower from spring to autumn and even in winter, although good light then becomes crucial. Propagation from cuttings is simple, too, once their needs are understood.

Grow them as large bushy plants 18–24 in (45–60 cm) tall. Plant several smaller plants in a tub or urn, or use them to contrast with a group of foliage plants, providing some brilliant colour to bring the group to life.

PELARGONIUM PELTATUM, the valued ivy-leaved geranium, is usually seen growing (perhaps among other plants) in a hanging basket or an ornamental urn. It needs good light and some sunshine to give of its best, but is otherwise not difficult.

Where circumstances permit, it can be grown into a much larger plant, perhaps trained on a trellis to form a mass of growth and dazzling flowers. This does, however, involve overwintering it successfully so it makes several years' growth. It is more usual to overwinter rooted cuttings or just buy in young plants each spring. But even where it must be treated as a temporary visitor, it can make a valuable contribution to interior decor.

Plants with flowers of various colours are available, from pink to scarlet, cherry-red and lavender, as well as the variegated-leaved variety 'L'Élégante', which has single pale mauve blooms.

CARE

LIGHT

Good light with several hours' sun per day.

TEMPERATURE

Warm 60–75°F (15–24°C) in summer; cooler 50–55°F (10–13°C) in winter. It can tolerate down to 45°F (7°C).

WATERING

Moderate while in active growth so that it never dries out, but so that the surface soil dries between waterings. Give the minimum to keep from parching in winter.

FEEDING

Liquid feed with high potash twice a month during active growth period.

COMPOST

Use soil-based mixture, perhaps with some extra peat to make more porous, and clay shards in the base of the pot for drainage. They seem to flower better if underpotted. Repot, giving fresh compost, each spring, or move into slightly larger container. Replace older plants with new ones from cuttings.

PROPAGATION

Stem cuttings 3–4 in (7.5–10 cm) long root within three weeks at any time during active season, although late summer/early autumn is the best. Use peat/sand mixture or soil-based compost with extra sand. Trim cutting just under a leaf joint, dip in rooting hormone, then insert by rim of pot. Keep warm, moderately well lit, moist but not too wet or humid (which would encourage blackleg disease).

Peperomia Species

PIPERACEAE

PEPEROMIAS of a number of different types and species are offered as house-plants. The three featured here are all good-tempered easy-to-manage plants with interestingly marked or coloured foliage and tail-like flower spikes.

Peperomia caperata, the Emerald Ripple, has bright green corrugated leaves carried on pink stalks, and makes a plant about 5–8 in (12.7–20 cm) tall. Its main dislike is over-watering which soon results in rotting leaves and leaf stalks. This apart, it is an easy plant. There is also a white-edged form called 'Variegata'.

P. argyreia, once known as *P. sandersii,* has smooth-surfaced rather fleshy leaves marked with alternate green and silver bands which radiate outwards from the leaf stalk. Its name *argyreia* means 'silvery'. Liking roughly the same conditions as *P. caperata,* it could be grown alongside it for a pleasant contrast of texture and colouring.

TOP AND RIGHT Peperomia argyreia.

ABOVE Peperomia caperata.

ABOVE RIGHT Peperomia magnolifolia *'Variegata'*.

— CARE —

LIGHT
Good light, but not intense sun, unless they are variegated.

TEMPERATURE
Normal warm room temperatures, 60–75°F (15–24°C); minimum 55°F (13°C). Ensure humid atmosphere without unduly wetting foliage by standing pots on trays of moist pebbles.

WATERING
As jungle floor plants they cannot abide drought, but overwatering rots them, so water moderately to keep compost just moist and let dry out partly between waterings.

FEEDING
Weak liquid feed monthly while in active growth.

COMPOST
Peperomias prefer peat-based compost and small pots because they do not make strong root systems. Only move one into a larger pot if obviously necessary.

PROPAGATION
P. caperata *and* P. argyreia *are usually rooted from leaf petiole cuttings (ie leaf with 1 in (2.5 cm) of stalk) inserted in slightly moist peat/sand mix. Stand in well-lit but not bright light in 65°F (18°C) and keep just moist. Should root and grow within two months. Root* P. magnoliifolia *from tip cuttings in similar conditions.*

P. magnoliifolia 'Variegata', the Desert Privet, has typical heart-shaped peperomia foliage but taller growth than the previous two plants. Its stems, 12 in (30 cm) tall or more, tend to flop and become creeping as it reaches maturity. Its form 'Variegata' is a green-and-gold-variegated plant, always sunny to look at, provided that it receives enough light to retain its full colouring.

All these peperomias will grow happily together to form a pleasant group, or among other contrasting foliage plants. They are nicely compact, and are therefore also suitable for bowls and bottle gardens.

Philodendron scandens

ARACEAE ▪ SWEETHEART VINE (OR HEARTLEAF PHILODENDRON)

1 For propagation, remove 3 – 4 in tip cuttings.

2 Dip base of stem in hormone rooting powder and insert three to five cuttings per 3½ in pot.

3 Insert two canes in pot for support.

4 Cover cuttings with clear plastic bag.

PHILODENDRON SCANDENS is a handsome glossy-leaved climbing plant of the arum family, grown entirely for its shapely heart-like leaves (it produces none of its arum flowers in the home).

In its native jungles it climbs trees, and so looks best and most authentic when trained up a moss pole into which its aerial roots can penetrate to draw nutriment and to use for anchorage. It can, however, be grown as a trailing pot or basket plant, although its vigorous growths then need to be trimmed back from time to time.

Given reasonable warmth (60°F/15°C or more) and light, this philodendron is easily managed. Wash dust and grime from its leaves regularly to get the best from its natural glossy appearance.

— CARE —

LIGHT
Give good light, but not direct sun.

TEMPERATURE
Normal warm temperatures, 55–75°F (13–24°C). This tropical plant cannot stand cooler temperatures.

WATERING
Moderate while actively growing; only enough to avoid drying out during winter rest period. Mist over in summer to provide necessary humidity.

FEEDING
Liquid feed twice monthly during season of active growth.

COMPOST
Use a mixture of equal-parts soil-based compost and peat. Move into a larger pot during active season when root growth demands it; top dress large plants.

PROPAGATION
Tip cuttings 3–4 in (7.5–10 cm) long, taken in late spring or early summer, root easily in a moist equal-parts mix of peat and sand in a pot covered with a plastic bag in a warm, fairly light position. They should be starting to grow after a month.

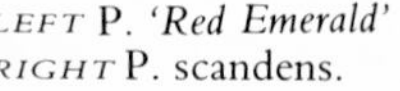

LEFT P. *'Red Emerald'*
RIGHT P. scandens.

Pilea cadierei

URTICACEAE ▪ ALUMINIUM PLANT

— CARE —

LIGHT
It likes dappled shade and strongly objects to bright sunlight.

TEMPERATURE
Keep warm, preferably 65–75°F (18–24°C), and never below 55°F (13°C). Revels in humid atmosphere too, so stand the pot on moist pebbles or plunge the pot in larger container of damp peat.

WATERING
Surprisingly it prefers moderate watering at all times, allowing surface compost to dry out between waterings, but it appreciates humid air.

FEEDING
Liquid feed in spring and summer only, about twice per month.

COMPOST
Use peat-based or equal-parts peat-based and soil-based mixture in a small pot (3½–4½ in/9–11.5 cm). Better to replace plants than to pot on when lower leaves fall in significant numbers.

PROPAGATION
Roots easily from stem tip cuttings 3 in (7.5 cm) long taken in spring. Trim just beneath leaf joint, dip in rooting hormone, then insert in mixture of 2 parts peat and 1 part sharp sand. Should root in about a month in a warm, shaded place if kept just moist.

PILEA CADIEREI, an attractive and very easily grown foliage plant from South-Eastern Asia, is known as the aluminium plant from the raised silvery markings on its rich green leaves, which represent its most distinctive feature. It contrasts well with other foliage plants, especially perhaps coleus.

It makes a bushy plant about 1 ft (30 cm) high at first, then tends to flop and spread unless its growths are pinched back or a selected compact form is grown. It may also start losing its lower leaves after a time, so it pays to propagate young plants as replacements (see care chart).

Platycerium bifurcatum

POLYPODIACEAE ▪ ELK'S HORN FERN

— CARE —

LIGHT
Good but not strong light.

TEMPERATURE
About 65°F (18°C) is ideal, rising to 75°F (24°C) in summer and not falling below 55°F (13°C) in winter. Mist-spray daily in warm dry conditions.

WATERING
Enough to keep compost really moist in summer warmth; considerably less in winter. If you cannot get water into the compost from a can, immerse the fern's roots in a bucket of water for 10 minutes when its limp fronds show this is necessary.

FEEDING
Little needed, but roots may be immersed in fertilizer solution a couple of times during a growing season.

COMPOST
Wrap roots in a mixture of coarse peat and sphagnum moss, and tie to a branch or a piece of wood with cotton. Plant will in time grip its host. Alternatively, grow in similar mixture in a hanging basket made of wooden slats.

PROPAGATION
From spores, but too difficult to do in the home.

PLATYCERIUM BIFURCATUM, a fern from the subtropical parts of Australia and the Polynesian islands, is a fascinating plant, by reason of its antler-like fronds and the way it is adapted to grow as an epiphyte on trees. In fact, it is not suitable for growing as a pot plant but prefers to be fixed to an old tree branch or a piece of wood. Wrap its roots in a mixture of peat and sphagnum moss, imitating the rotting tree leaves on which it subsists in nature. As a fern – a subtropical one at that – it does demand fairly humid conditions, so grow it where it can be misted over frequently if it is to thrive.

Its upper, branched fronds, the decorative ones, bear the spores from which this fern reproduces itself. The lower, sterile fronds grasp the branch or other host and serve to catch the leaves and other decomposing vegetation on which it lives.

Plumbago auriculata

PLUMBAGINACEAE ▪ CAPE LEADWORT

CARE

LIGHT
It demands full light and plenty of sun.

TEMPERATURE
Warm room temperatures, 60–75°F (15–24°C) in summer. Rest plant in winter at 45–50°F (7–10°C).

WATERING
Give plenty while growing to keep compost moist. Minimum to prevent parching in winter rest period.

FEEDING
Liquid feed with high potash twice monthly while in active growth to boost flowering.

COMPOST
Use soil-based mixture with some extra peat if necessary to prevent compaction. Move plant into larger pot in spring or top dress to give fresh nutriment.

SEASONAL CARE
In autumn gradually reduce watering as light levels decrease, until soil ball becomes quite dry, although not parched. Trim back all straggly growth. In spring, prune hard, shortening growth by two-thirds. Fresh shoots then spring from old wood to carry the new season's flowers. This also serves to keep the plant compact. Root 3–4 in (7.5–10 cm) semi-ripe stem cuttings in spring or summer in peat/sand mixture in small pots covered with plastic bags, or in closed propagator. Should root in about a month.

PLUMBAGO AURICULATA, still widely known as *P. capensis*, is by nature an untidy scrambling South African shrub, treasured nonetheless for its charming pale blue flowers. In greenhouses it is generally trained on a wall and pruned to keep it tidy and to encourage more flowers, which form on the young growth.

In the home it demands a light position and occasional pruning to keep it shapely, and so is best planted in a tub or urn located in a garden room or beside French doors. Apart from these strictures it is an easy plant to care for, and well worth the trouble to enjoy some of those plentiful clusters of pale blue flowers. It takes its name, plumbago, from the supposedly lead-blue colour of its blossoms.

Primula obconica

PRIMULACEAE ▪ GERMAN PRIMROSE (OR POISON PRIMROSE)

—CARE—

LIGHT
Good light with some sun, although not scorching sun.

TEMPERATURE
Primulas prefer cooler temperatures, 50–60°F (1–15°C). Stand pots on trays of moist pebbles to provide extra humidity to discourage red spider mite attack and extend life of blooms.

WATERING
Generous, but not so as to be waterlogged.

FEEDING
Liquid feed fortnightly while making blooms.

COMPOST
Soil-based compost with a little extra peat and without lime.

SEASONAL CARE
To flower this primula for a second season, keep it growing after blooming to rebuild its strength. Top dress with fresh compost in early autumn, ready for winter/spring flowering. Water with magnesium sulphate solution if yellowing leaves indicate shortage of magnesium.

BELOW *Like the pelargoniums, primulas look fine in groups with different coloured flowers.*

PRIMULA OBCONICA, a Chinese species, is one of several kinds grown as pot plants, and by far the most resilient. Its clusters of 1 in (2.5 cm) diameter flowers may be rich magenta-red, pink, salmon, white or pale blue, and are long-lasting. It has a long flowering season, often blooming from late winter to early summer and again in autumn.

To extend the flowering season, plants can be raised from seeds in late summer and also in spring to give blooms in spring and late summer. Potted plants are widely marketed.

The plant's one drawback is its hairy leaves, to which some people with sensitive skins are allergic.

This apart, it is a most useful flowering plant, contributing colour to the home for many months of the year.

Pteris cretica

POLYPODIACEAE ▪ CRETAN BRAKE (OR RIBBON FERN)

—CARE—

LIGHT
Give good light all year, but not fierce sun.

TEMPERATURE
Normal warm room temperatures, 60–75°F (15–24°C) in summer, 55–65°F (13–18°C) in winter. Balance with extra humidity at higher temperatures.

WATERING
Like most ferns must always be kept moist. Give plenty of water in summer, less in cooler winter temperatures.

FEEDING
Give weak liquid feed monthly while actively growing.

COMPOST
Use soil-based mixture with equal amount of peat, or a peat-based mixture. Move plants into larger pots in spring if root growth demands it.

SEASONAL CARE
Divide large mature plants in spring, cutting rhizome (just beneath soil surface) with a sharp knife. Pot well rooted pieces in small (3½ in/9 cm) pots. Trim away old worn-out fronds as necessary.

PTERIS CRETICA, a tender fern from Crete, as its name indicates, makes a neat bushy foliage pot plant some 8 in (20 cm) tall and remains decorative if not particularly remarkable the year round given the conditions it likes. These are mainly adequate warmth (55–70°F/13–21°C), water and humidity, and good but not bright light.

The form known as 'Albo-lineata', which has a creamy white band beside the midrib of each pinna (sub-division of a frond, equivalent to a leaflet), is more eye-catching and therefore more suitable as a specimen plant than as a pleasant filler between other plants. Like most variegated plants, however, it is not such a strong grower as the plain green *P. cretica*.

Rhipsalidopsis gaertneri

CACTACEAE ▪ EASTER CACTUS

ABOVE AND BELOW Rhipsalidopsis gaertneri. *BOTTOM Variety of the Easter Cactus, 'Laura Ann'.*

CARE

LIGHT
As plants of the forest they like moderate light. In fierce sun their stems turn yellow and may shrivel. Give them an outdoor holiday in the summer, but in a shady spot.

TEMPERATURE
They are happy at 60–70°F (15–21°C) throughout the year, and tolerate temperatures a little above and below this, but no lower than 50°F (10°C).

WATERING
Plenty to ensure the compost is really moist (although not soggy) from early spring until flowering is over. Give the minimum to keep the plant from drying out in the next two or three weeks rest period, then water moderately for the remainder of the year. Restrict watering if temperature falls below 60°F (15°C), or the plant could rot at soil level.

FEEDING
Give a high-potash fertilizer twice a month in spring as soon as flower buds form until blooming is finished. Discontinue this during the plant's short rest period, then resume if growing in a peat-based compost, but not in a soil-based compost which already contains sufficient nutriment.

COMPOST
Soil-based or peat-based, the latter preferred, particularly for hanging baskets in which this plant's arching growth looks particularly decorative. Add 1 part gritty sand to 3 parts of peat-based mixture to help drainage.

PROPAGATION
Simple, using single or pairs of stem segments, inserted upright in usual potting compost in spring or summer. Keep warm and water moderately like mature plants, but no special treatment required. Should root in about six weeks.

RHIPSALIDOPSIS GAERTNERI, the so-called Easter cactus, because spring is its usual flowering time, is a jungle cactus that naturally grows in rotted vegetation in trees in the tropical rain forest of South America, and *not* in the desert. This, of course, has a strong bearing on how it should be cared for.

The stems of this plant, which can grow about 1 ft (30 cm) across, are formed of flat segments, each about 1½ in (3.8 cm) long. It forms its brick-red flowers singly or in small clusters at the tips of its stems. Individual blooms last but a day or two, but the display goes on for several weeks.

The daintier *R. rosea* is smaller in all its parts, being about half the diameter of its relative, and bears pretty pink flowers in spring.

Rhoicissus rhomboidea

VITACEAE ▪ GRAPE IVY (OR NATURAL VINE)

—*CARE*—

LIGHT
Good light with some sun, but not fierce sunshine.

TEMPERATURE
Warm room temperatures in summer – 60–75°F (15–24°C) – but benefits from cooler conditions, 50–55°F (10–13°C) in winter to encourage it to rest.

WATERING
Moderate throughout growing season; just enough to keep moist in winter.

FEEDING
Liquid feed fortnightly while growing.

COMPOST
Soil-based mix. Move plants into larger pots or top dress as necessary.

PROPAGATION
Root tip cuttings in moist peat/sand mix in spring or summer, covering with a plastic bag. Should root within a month.

R HOICISSUS RHOMBOIDEA is a glossy-leaved creeper used, like its relative *Cissus antarctica*, for clothing a trellis or for training over various kinds of support. The plant is, in fact, now more correctly called *Cissus rhombifolia*, although its former name still remains more popular.

It differs from *C. antarctica* mainly in the shape of its leaves, each formed of three leaflets of rhomboid shape; hence its name. It climbs on its own by means of tendrils. Its widely marketed form 'Ellen Danica' is superior, with larger leaflets.

Rochea coccinea

CRASSULACEAE ▪ CRASSULA

— CARE —

LIGHT
It enjoys direct sun. If light is poor, growth becomes loose and weak.

TEMPERATURE
It is happy in summer room temperatures of 60–75°F (15–24°C), but ensure a cooler winter rest period at 45–55°F (7–13°C). It appreciates an outdoor holiday in summer, screened from the fiercest sun.

WATERING
Moderate in summer, so that compost is kept moist, although the surface layer should dry out between waterings. Give the minimum to keep from drying out in winter rest period, so that growth is not forced.

FEEDING
Give high-potash fertilizer twice a month from first sign of flower buds until flowering is over.

COMPOST
Use soil-based potting mixture (2 parts) with extra 1 part of sharp sand for free drainage. Move plants into larger pots in spring if necessary. Discard any which have become leafless at the base.

SEASONAL CARE
Stems that have borne flowers should be cut back when blooms fade.
Rochea coccinea *is easily propagated from stem cuttings in spring or summer. Take top 3–4 in (7.5–10 cm) of a branch; remove lower leaves, and insert in rochea potting mixture after leaving to dry for a couple of days. It should root within a month.*

ROCHEA COCCINEA is a neat, rather rigid-growing succulent cultivated mainly for its scarlet flowers which open in midsummer although nurserymen often force them into bloom in spring. Treated like any other succulent, it is an easily-managed plant, and is colourful for 3–4 weeks.

The bushy plants develop six or more upright stems covered in regularly-arranged, triangular, leathery green leaves. The flowers, which are also sweetly scented, are carried in clusters at the tops of these stems. There are also white and red-and-white flowered forms of this rochea.

Saintpaulia ionantha

GESNERIACEAE ▪ AFRICAN VIOLET

ABOVE The original S. ionantha.

BELOW S. ionantha *'Rococo'*.

BELOW RIGHT Saintpaulia orbicularia.

SAINTPAULIA IONANTHA, the familiar and much treasured African violet, might appear to some people to be far from resilient – temperamental indeed. But, given the conditions it demands (which are not too difficult to provide in most homes), it should thrive and flower for many months of the year. Leaf cuttings root quite easily too, so a succession of vigorous young plants can be kept going for years.

This plant comes from Tanzania, near the equator, so it needs warmth to live happily in the home – a minimum of 60°F (15°C), and preferably nearer 70–75°F (21–24°C). It also demands high humidity, provided that the temperature is quite high. (In cool and humid conditions, fungus disease could gain a hold.) Linked with its liking for warmth, it also hates draughts, so stand the plant where it is protected from air currents.

In shade, an African violet is unlikely to flower, but although it likes good light, it must not be placed in fierce sunshine or its soft, fleshy leaves may be scorched and the plant become sickly.

Watering is a matter of care. It must be adequate yet moderate, so that the crown of the plant does not rot. Water must be kept off the soft hairy leaves or they will be marked. Lift the lower leaves when watering to keep water off the plant itself. Occasionally water the plant from below instead.

There is now a wide range of fine hybrids on sale, with blooms varying from pale mauve to deep violet, as well as pink, purple-pink and white, bicolors, and blooms with white-edged petals. There are also exquisite miniatures in several colours which make charming feature plants, such as in a large brandy glass or other suitable container. In fact, a glass container provides an African violet with just the warm humid, draught-free conditions it enjoys.

—*CARE*—

LIGHT
Good light without strong sunshine. A west-facing window is best in summer. Artificial light to extend day-length to 14 hrs is essential to get flowers in winter.

TEMPERATURE
Warm, 60–75°F (15–24°C) with 60°F (15°C) the minimum winter temperature. Plants can nonetheless survive slightly lower levels if compost is kept dry.

WATERING
Enough to keep compost moist, but leave to partly dry out between waterings to avoid the risk of rotting.

FEEDING
Give very weak liquid feed at each watering to keep in vigorous health.

COMPOST
They prefer a peat-based mixture with an equivalent amount of coarse sand or perlite to provide sharp drainage.

PROPAGATION
Take leaf cuttings with 2 in (5 cm) of leaf stalk attached. Trim back to 1½ in (3.8 cm) long and insert ½ in (1.3 cm) deep in peat/sand mix; cover with plastic bag. Should take about two months to form tiny plantlets at base of leaf stalk.

SEASONAL CARE
Watch for signs of infestation by mealy bugs, whitefly or aphids, particularly during the warmer months.

Sanchezia nobilis

ACANTHACEAE

SANCHEZIA NOBILIS makes quite a large plant, grown primarily for its handsome striped foliage, although it does also produce spikes of yellow flowers in autumn. The oval pointed leaves, mid-green with yellow or off-white veins, clothe this often 3 ft (90 cm) tall plant right to soil level. Its one key demand is for high humidity, for it is subtropical.

The flower clusters rise above the foliage and carry many 2 in (5 cm) long tubular blooms. Sanchezia is a relative of the Zebra Plant, aphelandra, its similarity to which is quite marked. If this plant outgrows its space, prune it back in spring.

— CARE —

LIGHT
Good light with some sun, although not fierce sun.

TEMPERATURE
Warm room temperatures in summer 60–75°F (15–24°C); somewhat cooler in winter, with a minimum of 55°F (13°C).

WATERING
Generous in summer to keep moist; more restrained in winter.

FEEDING
Liquid feed fortnightly while actively growing.

COMPOST
Soil-based mixture. Move into larger pots as necessary, possibly more than once in a season; top dress mature plants. It is best to replace old plants every second year.

PROPAGATION
Root side-shoot cuttings from near top of plant in summer in moist peat/sand mix after treating with hormone rooting preparation. Cover with a plastic bag to maintain humidity. Should root within six weeks.

Sansevieria trifasciata 'Laurentii'

AGAVACEAE ▪ MOTHER-IN-LAW'S TONGUE (OR SNAKESKIN PLANT)

CARE

LIGHT
Prefers bright light and plenty of sun, although it tolerates slight shade. Stops growing in poor light.

TEMPERATURE
As a semi-desert plant from Southern Africa it prefers 65–80°F (18–27°C) in summer; a little less, although not below 55°F (13°C), in winter, because of the risk of rotting.

WATERING
Moderate while in active growth, leaving to partly dry out between waterings. Give a minimum to keep just moist during midwinter period.

FEEDING
Half-strength liquid feed once a month during active season only.

COMPOST
Use 2 parts soil-based potting compost with 1 part gritty sand to ensure free drainage, aided by a generous layer of broken pieces of clay pot in the base of the container. Use a clay pot for any large plant, which could overbalance in a light plastic one. Repot only when the pot is crammed with growth and demands it. Do this in spring.

PROPAGATION
The 'Laurentii' form must be increased by removing offsets (leaf clusters 6 in/15 cm high), probably with roots already forming, and setting in normal potting mix, supported by a small cane if necessary. In warm 65–70°F (18–21°C) conditions, moderate light and restrained watering, these should root and become established within a month.

Propagate T. trifasciata *itself from leaf cuttings, 2 in (5 cm) lengths of leaf inserted right-way-up in peat/sand mixture in similar conditions to offsets. Shoots eventually grow from the cuttings, which go on to form small plants.*

SANSEVIERIA TRIFASCIATA 'Laurentii', the well-known and widely grown Mother-in-Law's Tongue, is one of the toughest and least destructible of all house-plants. It withstands drought without harm, rarely needs potting, and always looks handsome and a cheerful colour. Its main enemies are low winter temperatures and excessive watering, particularly when it is cold, either of which can cause rotting of its rhizomes (the thick stems at soil level from which the leaves spring).

A bold potful of this sansevieria, with perhaps three plants together, can make an eye-catching feature. Alternatively, a single plant can be associated with other foliage plants of contrasting shape to make a balanced and interesting group. In the latter case, make sure the sansevieria is not overwatered.

'Laurentii' is a yellow-edged form of the species *S. trifasciata*, which has green leaves characterized by the snakeskin banding.

Saxifraga stolonifera

SAXIFRAGACEAE ▪ MOTHER OF THOUSANDS

—CARE—

LIGHT
Give good light, but only limited periods of bright sun. 'Tricolor' needs more sun to maintain good growth and coloration.

TEMPERATURE
A tolerant plant happy in cool atmosphere of 50–60°F (10–15°C), although tolerates it up to 75°F (24°C) in summer if high humidity is provided. Minimum of 40°F (4°C) in winter. Keep 'Tricolor' within 60–70°F (15–21°C) all year if possible.

WATERING
Give plenty to ensure that compost is really moist from early spring to end of flowering, then gradually reduce. Give just enough in rest period to keep from drying out.

FEEDING
Liquid feed once a month in season of active growth.

COMPOST
Use soil-based potting mixture with ¾ in (1.9 cm) layer of drainage material in base. Move plants into larger pots in spring, but discard and replace after several seasons.

PROPAGATION
Use the plant's bounty of plantlets. Detach them and plant in small pots of peat/sand mixture, or pin plantlets to surface of similar compost while attached to parent and sever after well rooted – about 4–6 weeks. Give them filtered light, 65–70°F (18–21°C) and restrained watering until rooted.

SAXIFRAGA STOLONIFERA is a modest-sized foliage plant grown primarily for the colouring of its leaves and for its many similar plantlets which hang on long wiry stems 9 in–3 ft (22.5–90 cm) long, although it does also produce tiny, starry white flowers on long stems in late summer.

This plant grows no more than 9 in (22.5 cm) tall and perhaps 15 in (37.5 cm) across, but when carrying six, ten, or more babies makes a much larger specimen. Its habit of growth fits it for a hanging pot — a hanging basket, unless of unusually small size, is too wide for it — or a position on a shelf or pedestal where its plantlets can hang freely.

Its leaves are a dark olive-green, their veins picked out in silver-green, and are beetroot red on the reverse with hairy red stalks while young. It is an easily pleased plant. There is also a more colourful but less vigorous variegated form, 'Tricolor', with creamy edges to its leaves, which are often suffused with pink in bright light.

ABOVE Saxifraga stolonifera *'Tricolor' is not as vigorous as the unvariegated plant.*

Schlumbergera bridgesii

CACTACEAE ▪ CHRISTMAS CACTUS

— CARE —

LIGHT
Moderate from partly shaded window in summer. Winter light intensity suits it. Give plant short-day treatment if necessary to get flowers by covering with black plastic through autumn and early winter.

TEMPERATURE
Ordinary warm room temperatures, 60–75°F (15–24°C) winter and summer, suit this plant. Give it an outdoor holiday in summer, in shade.

WATERING
Water plentifully throughout year, except during the short rest period after flowering, to keep compost moist and stems growing. Use soft (lime-free) water. Mist with water in spring and summer to keep humid.

FEEDING
Give high-potash liquid feed twice a month, except during rest period.

COMPOST
It prefers 3 parts peat-based compost with 1 part of coarse sand or perlite to aid drainage. Suited to a hanging basket lined with sphagnum moss. Or use a smallish pot in scale with its small root system.

PROPAGATION
Root stem cuttings consisting of two or three segments in recommended potting mixture in spring or summer. Let cutting dry for some hours, then insert upright in compost, or several round rim of 3 in (7.5 cm) pot. Should root within a month.

SCHLUMBERGERA BRIDGESII, the much-loved Christmas cactus, gives rise to many disappointments and questions because its needs are too rarely understood. It is vital to realize that it is a jungle cactus that lives in rotted vegetation in the crotches of forest trees, *not* a desert cactus adapted to parched conditions. This has a radical bearing on caring for the plant.

It should also be remembered that its flowering is triggered by short day-length. So if the hours of light it receives in winter are extended by standing in an artificially lit room, flowering is naturally suppressed.

The Christmas cactus is distinguished by the rounded notches to its stem segments. Plants with spiky-looking notches have been developed from *S. truncata* and are often smaller. *S. bridgesii* grows about 1 ft (30 cm) across with segments about 1½ in (3.8 cm) long and ½ in (1.3 cm) or a little more across. The rich magenta-pink blooms, each lasting about three days, are about 1½ in (3.8 cm) across and 2½ in (5.3 cm) long. A plant's display can last about three weeks.

Despite its popular name, this plant does not always flower at Christmas, although nurserymen can manipulate conditions so that it does. In the home it can flower early and be over by Christmas, or open long after – or even bloom at both these times. This is triggered by water supply, warmth and the number of hours of daylight, *not* by the calendar. Where necessary, stand your plant in an unlit room in autumn, or gently cover it in the evening with a sheet of black plastic.

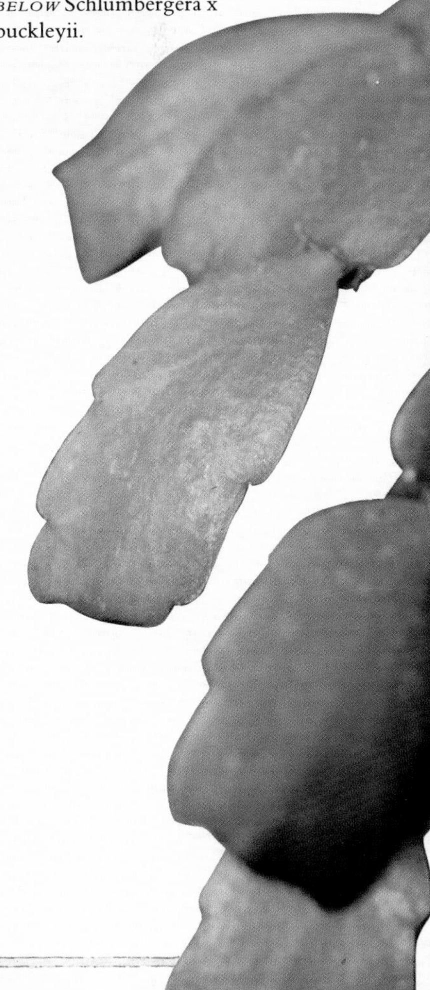

BELOW Schlumbergera x buckleyii.

Scindapsus aureus

ARACEAE ▪ DEVIL'S IVY (OR POTHOS)

CARE

LIGHT
Bright light essential to retain good leaf colouring.

TEMPERATURE
Normal summer room temperatures, 60–75°F (15–24°C); about 60°F (15°C) in winter, with minimum of 50°F (10°C). Provide atmospheric humidity around plants by standing containers on tray of moist pebbbles.

WATERING
Moderate in summer to keep moist; barely moist in winter.

FEEDING
Liquid feed fortnightly while in active growth.

COMPOST
Soil-based mixture with small proportion of extra peat. Move plants into larger pots each spring; top dress larger plants.

PROPAGATION
Root 3–4 in (7.5–10 cm) long stem cuttings in moist peat/sand mix in spring. Remove lower leaves, dip in hormone rooting preparation, insert, and enclose in plastic bag. Should root within six weeks.

SCINDAPSUS AUREUS, now more correctly known as *Epipremnum aureum*, is a trailing plant of the arum family from Polynesia. It is usually grown in a hanging basket, although it could be trained to a moss pole. It can grow 4–6 ft (1.2–1.8 m) long, but may be pruned to keep it more compact if necessary.

Its evergreen leaves are irregularly splashed with gold, but there are other forms with more gold in the leaves; the variety 'Marble Queen' has white and green marbled foliage.

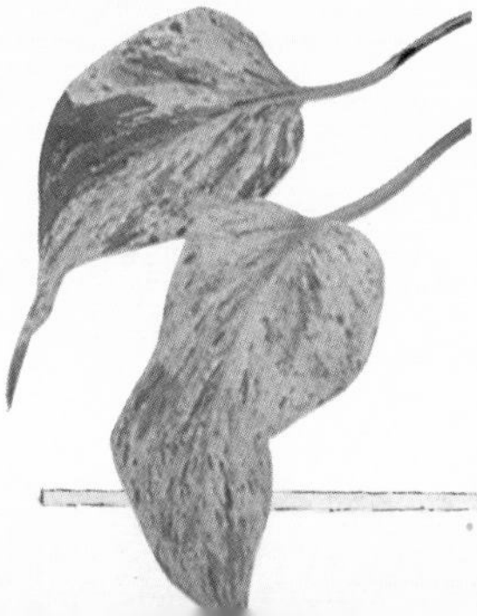

Sedums

CRASSULACEAE ▪ STONECROPS

Many of the numerous species of sedum make attractive, interesting, easily-pleased house plants, particularly for windowsills. (They demand good light to thrive). Three of contrasting habit are featured here: all need similar care.

Sedum sieboldii is a tough, fairly hardy succulent plant that originated in Japan. The form known as 'Medio-variegatum' is much more decorative, its fleshy blue-green leaves are splashed in the centre with cream and often tinged pink as well.

This plant grows only 3–4 in (7.5–10 cm) high, but its pendant stems can hang down some 8 in (20 cm) if it is grown in a hanging basket or in a pot suspended on wires – the best way to display it. The clusters of tiny pink flowers that form at the ends of its stems in late summer are insignificant, but the plant's graceful habit of growth and colourful foliage are sufficient to earn it a place in the home.

Sedum rubrotinctum, sometimes known as Christmas Cheer, is again grown for its colourful foliage, in this case green heavily tinted with red if it is kept warm and dry. The succulent leaves that form on its thin 4–6 in (10–15 cm) tall stems are plump and not unlike jelly beans. Taller stems tend to fall over and root into the compost in which the plant is growing. This sedum rarely flowers indoors.

Sedum morganianum, from Mexico, is another pendant plant, but much more vigorous than *S. sieboldii*. Each of its hanging stems, which can extend from 18 in to 3 ft (45–90 cm) in length, is clothed in fleshy grey-blue leaves which overlap each other to form 'donkey's tails', the plant's familiar name. It does not readily flower indoors because the light is not strong enough, but when it does the flowers are pink and appear in early spring.

—CARE—

LIGHT
Give good light in full sun for good colouring.

TEMPERATURE
Warm room temperatures 60–75°F (15–24°C) in summer; 45–50°F (7–10°C) in winter rest period.

WATERING
Moderate while in growth, allowing to partly dry out between waterings. Minimum in winter to keep from parching.

FEEDING
None necessary.

COMPOST
Use soil-based mixture with extra half part of coarse sand or perlite added for sharp drainage. Move plants into larger pots in spring if development demands.

PROPAGATION
Root 3–4 in (7.5–10 cm) long stem cuttings in spring or summer, after stripping away lower leaves and leaving to dry for a couple of days. Should be growing within a month.

ABOVE Sedum morganianum.

BELOW LEFT Sedum rubrotinctum.

BELOW Sedum sieboldii *'Medio Variegata'*.

Setcreasea purpurea

COMMELINACEAE ▪ PURPLE HEART

—*CARE*—

LIGHT
Good light, including some direct sunlight.

TEMPERATURE
It revels in warm temperatures 65–75°F (18–24°C) but can survive much lower ones to 45°F (7°C).

WATERING
Moderate, so that it does not go without water, but fairly dry between waterings.

FEEDING
Liquid feed monthly while in active growth.

COMPOST
Use soil-based mixture. Move into larger pot in spring, possibly also in late summer, for this is a quick grower. Discard rangy, bare-stemmed plants and replace from cuttings.

SEASONAL CARE
Root from 3 in (7.5 cm) long stem cuttings in spring or summer in potting mixture, after removing lower leaves. Stand pots of cuttings in filtered light, and water with restraint.

Handle this plant's leaves as little as possible so their attractive bloom is not disturbed.

SETCREASEA PURPUREA is a fleshy-leaved trailing plant, closely related to the familiar trailing tradescantia, grown for its handsome purple colouring. It needs a sunny spot to maintain its richest leaf colour, and a container such as a hanging pot or basket from which it can trail freely.

Although its wandering stems can be cut back to suit available space, cutting should be undertaken sensitively so that the essential character of the plant is not lost.

It does open tiny magenta-pink three-petalled flowers in midsummer, but these are not large enough or profuse enough to be showy.

Spathiphyllum wallisii

ARACEAE ▪ PEACE LILY

—*CARE*—

LIGHT
Moderate, never direct sun.

TEMPERATURE
Warm, 60–75°F (15–24°C); a minimum of 55°F (13°C).

WATERING
Moderate while growing and temperatures are above 60°F (15°C). Just enough to keep moist at lower temperatures. Mist foliage every few days at higher temperatures to deter red spider mite.

FEEDING
Liquid feed twice monthly while actively growing.

COMPOST
Use soil-based mixture with extra peat and sharp sand, or peat-based mix. Move into larger pot in spring when root development demands.

PROPAGATION
Divide mature clumps, potting pieces with several leaves, a section of rhizome and some feeding roots. Water with restraint until established.

SPATHIPHYLLUM WALLISII, a glossy-leaved tropical evergreen, is grown partly for its pleasant foliage and partly for its white arum-like flowers, which develop in spring or summer. The spathes change from white to green after a week or so, but remain decorative for several more weeks before they need removing.

This is a plant for a somewhat shady position in a warm room between 55 and 75°F (13–24°C), but is remarkably tolerant for a tropical plant. Keep the air around it humid in order to compensate the plant for its desire for its natural jungle environment.

Streptocarpus 'Constant Nymph'

GESNERIACEAE ▪ CAPE PRIMROSE

STREPTOCARPUS 'Constant Nymph' is the most prolific flowering of the many hybrids grown for home and conservatory decoration. Other hybrids produce larger, more striking flowers, but in nowhere near the quantities 'Constant Nymph' provides in the course of a season.

This is a good-tempered plant provided that its few basic needs are respected. First, its leaves are notoriously brittle and easily damaged, so stand the plant where it is unlikely to be knocked. Then to thrive it needs good light, although not fierce sun, moderate watering and humidity, and normal room temperatures. It is not a deep-rooted plant, so a pan or half-pot could be preferable to a full-depth pot.

Where it is happy, a streptocarpus can flower off and on throughout the warmer months from spring to early autumn. 'Constant Nymph' is a lovely mauve-blue with dark blue lines running back into the blooms' cream throats.

Two of the many Streptocarpus hybrids now available; you may prefer the hybrids because their leaves are far less brittle than the original S. *'Constant Nymph'.*

CARE

LIGHT
Good light but not strong sun. Moderate light in winter.

TEMPERATURE
Normal warm room temperatures, 60–75°F (15–24°C); provide extra humidity at high temperatures by standing container on moist pebbles. Below 55°F (13°C) in winter, plants become dormant and should then be kept much drier or they could rot.

WATERING
Moderate, allowing surface to dry out between waterings. Excess could rot roots.

FEEDING
Give weak feed twice monthly while in active growth only.

COMPOST
It prefers a peaty mixture made up of 2 parts coarse peat to 3 parts coarse sand or perlite in order to keep the mixture porous. Add some lime to sweeten it. Only move plants to larger pots when obviously necessary. Use shallow containers.

PROPAGATION
Root leaf cuttings. Select a healthy leaf and cut it across into several 3–4 in (7.5–10 cm) long sections. Insert the end of each (making sure they are right-way-up) in recommended potting mixture, and keep slightly moist. Plantlets should form within six weeks at the base of each cutting. Allow these to develop until 2 in (5 cm) high and robust enough to be potted separately.

Tolmiea menziesii

SAXIFRAGACEAE ▪ PIGGY-BACK PLANT (OR YOUTH ON AGE)

ABOVE T. menziesii *usually develop into a more compact specimen than this, more like the rounded shape shown below.*

TOLMIEA MENZIESII forms a pleasant, bushy foliage plant some 12 in (30 cm) tall and 15 in (37.5 cm) across , which is grown primarily for its fascinating habit of forming plantlets on its mature leaves. These appear just where the leaf blade joins the stalk. Pressing the leaf down by their weight, they readily root into whatever soil they contact. They thus provide a ready means of propagation for home gardeners.

This plant is easy to please, although it needs a minimum of 50°F (10°C) and must not be allowed to become too dry or it could become infested by red spider mite. Its deeply-toothed heart-shaped leaves and intriguing plantlets give it interest.

—CARE—

LIGHT
Give good or moderate light, although it adapts to some shade.

TEMPERATURE
It is tolerant between a minimum of 50°F (10°C) and 75°F (24°C), but ensure extra humidity at higher temperatures.

WATERING
Moderate while actively growing, allowing to partly dry out between waterings. Minimum to keep just moist during midwinter rest.

FEEDING
Liquid feed fortnightly while actively growing.

COMPOST
Use soil-based mixture, perhaps with some extra peat to keep porous. Move into larger container when root growth demands. Group several plants in pot or hanging basket for bold display.

PROPAGATION
Root some of plantlets in spring or summer. Cut away leaf bearing plantlet with 1 in (2.5 cm) of stalk, and insert in equal-parts peat/sand mix so that plantlet touches compost surface. Keep warm, just moist and moderately lit, and it should root within three weeks. Alternatively, pin down suitable leaf in small pot while attached to parent plant so plantlet roots. It can then be severed from original plant. Plantlets develop into ornamental plants within six months.

Tradescantia fluminensis

COMMELINACEAE ▪ SPEEDY JENNY

— CARE —

LIGHT
Give good light, including some sun, for healthy growth and bright colouring.

TEMPERATURE
Warm room temperatures, 65–75°F (18–24°C), a minimum of 55°F (13°C), because fleshy leaves are vulnerable to cold.

WATERING
Generous during active growth in order to keep compost moist. With restraint when plants are semi-dormant.

FEEDING
Liquid feed twice a month during season of active growth.

COMPOST
Use soil-based mixture with extra peat or sand added if necessary to keep porous. Move plants into larger pots during active season when root growth indicates necessary. Discard old plants.

PROPAGATION
Root 3 in (7.5 cm) tip cuttings in small pot of moist peat/sand mixture in a warm place (70°F/21°C) in diffused light. Should root in a fortnight. Also root in water. Pot these carefully to avoid root damage.

TRADESCANTIA FLUMINENSIS 'Variegata' and its stronger-growing form 'Quicksilver', both of which have green and white striped leaves, are surely the most popular of all indoor hanging basket or suspended pot plants. They grow freely, are cheerfully coloured and can easily be propagated. Yet many plants of this type fall far short of perfection, for this plant does need good light to produce well-clothed stems with full-coloured variegation. Its leaves soon turn brown at the tips, or altogether, if it dries out, and it also dislikes over-watering. Despite this, it is generally undemanding — but its few basic needs must be respected.

Tip cuttings 3 in (7.5 cm) long root at any time from spring to autumn, even in water. This plant is therefore acquired more often from friends than from a florist or garden centre. Grow four or more rooted cuttings to a pot to produce a bold display of colourful leaves. Nip out the tips of the shoots when they become straggly to keep the plant tidy and to encourage branching nearer the centre (for it has a tendency to become bare there). Replace exhausted plants with rooted cuttings as often as necessary.

TOP Tradescantia fluminensis *'Variegata', and the sturdier 'Quicksilver' (above and right).*

Vallota speciosa

AMARYLLIDACEAE ▪ SCARBOROUGH LILY

— CARE —

LIGHT
Good light and some sunshine.

TEMPERATURE
Normal summer room temperatures, 60–75°F (15–24°C). Cooler during winter rest 50–55°F (10–13°C).

WATERING
Sparingly during winter rest period and for newly potted bulbs. Enough in summer to keep compost moist.

FEEDING
Liquid feed fortnightly with balanced formula from spring to midsummer. Then change to high-potash feed until flowering is over. No feed thereafter.

PROPAGATION
Divide clumps of bulbs and pot separately. Move into gradually larger pots until they reach flowering size.

VALLOTA SPECIOSA, popularly known as the Scarborough lily because bulbs are said to have been washed up on the northern English coast there after a shipwreck, is a pleasant scarlet-flowered bulb from South Africa. It is rather like a smaller hippeastrum, bearing anything from three to eight small trumpets on each 2 ft (60 cm) stem.

The bulbs tend to multiply quite profusely, so providing a ready means of starting extra pots of this lily. There are also pink-and white-flowered forms, but these are rarely offered for sale.

Vriesia splendens

BROMELIACEAE ▪ FLAMING SWORD

—CARE—

LIGHT
Good light and sunshine, but not the fiercest midday sun.

TEMPERATURE
Normal warm room temperatures, 60–75°F (15–24°C); humidity should be provided by standing the container on a tray of moist pebbles.

WATERING
Fill central vase with soft water so it overflows into potting mixture during active growth. Keep barely moist during winter rest.

COMPOST
Equal-parts mix of peat, sharp sand and soil-based mixture. Pot loosely.

FEEDING
Weak liquid feed monthly.

PROPAGATION
Detach and root offsets when 4–6 in (10–15 cm) long in peat/sand mix in warm place (70°F/21°C), covered with plastic bag. Should root within six weeks.

VRIESIA SPLENDENS, when in bloom, is one of the showiest of the bromeliads (pineapple family). A tree-dwelling species from the forests of northern South America, it forms the typical bromeliad 'vase', a reservoir for moisture and, in the wild, a home for tree frogs, insects and other creatures which, when they die there, help to feed the plant with the nitrogen and other materials it needs.

Its cross-banded leaves are interesting, but when it is perhaps five years old it produces a 1½–2 ft (45–60 cm) tall flower stem from the centre of its leaf rosette. This bears a brilliant red sword-shaped cluster of bracts from which rather insignificant yellow flowers develop. They are short-lived, but the bracts, for which the plant is cultivated, remain decorative for several months.

Yucca elephantipes

AGAVACEAE ▪ SPINELESS YUCCA

— CARE —

LIGHT
Good light with sunshine is essential.

TEMPERATURE
Normal warm room temperatures 60–75°F (15–24°C), but it tolerates winter temperatures down to 50°F (10°C).

WATERING
As necessary to keep compost moist in summer. Sparing in winter to encourage rest.

FEEDING
Liquid feed monthly while actively growing.

COMPOST
Soil-based compost and clay pot to avoid a top-heavy plant falling over. Top dress or move to larger pot in spring as necessary.

SEASONAL CARE
Give plant an outdoor holiday in summer in a sunny spot.
Propagate from offsets, if any, removing when they have several leaves about 8 in (20 cm) long. Use equal-parts soil-based mix and sharp sand.

YUCCA ELEPHANTIPES, unlike the yuccas grown outdoors in temperate zones, are not spiny but have soft foliage of similar shape. As indoor plants they are frequently grown from Ti logs — lengths of woody stem 1–1½ in (2.5–3.8 cm) thick which sprout to form side-shoots at the top. In this form they are more convenient both to market and to accommodate in rooms.

The name *elephantipes* refers to the thickened base of the stem of a naturally-grown plant, which does indeed resemble an elephant's foot.

This plant brings an exotic flavour to the room's decor, but in this form it is purely a foliage plant, never growing large or mature enough to bloom.

Zebrina pendula

COMMELINACEAE ▪ WANDERING JEW (OR SILVERY INCH PLANT)

CARE

LIGHT
It likes good light and sun to display rich colour.

TEMPERATURE
Normal warm room temperatures 60–75°F (15–24°C), but it can tolerate cooler temperatures down to 55°F (13°C).

WATERING
Moderate while growing, just enough to keep slightly moist while resting in winter.

FEEDING
Liquid feed fortnightly while actively growing.

COMPOST
Use a soil-based mix, perhaps with a little extra peat to keep porous. Put several cuttings to each pot, perhaps a dozen to a basket.

PROPAGATION
Root 3 in (7.5 cm) tip cuttings during active growing season in moist sand/peat mix or in water. Slowly adapt them to normal compost, watering and pot size.

ZEBRINA PENDULA is a fleshy-leaved trailing plant from Mexico, a close relative of the even more familiar tradescantia, which shares its common name of Wandering Jew because of its extensive growth. Zebrina is also well named for its distinctly striped leaves which have a green central stripe and green edges with silvery-white areas between.

In addition to the species itself there are more colourful forms, including 'Purpusii' with purple-bronze leaves, and 'Quadricolor' striped in pink, cream, green and silver. All are fine in hanging baskets or pots from which their growth can cascade. They need occasional pruning back to keep them tidy, good light, and enough water to keep them moist, but are otherwise undemanding.

Index

Page references in *italic* refer to captions.

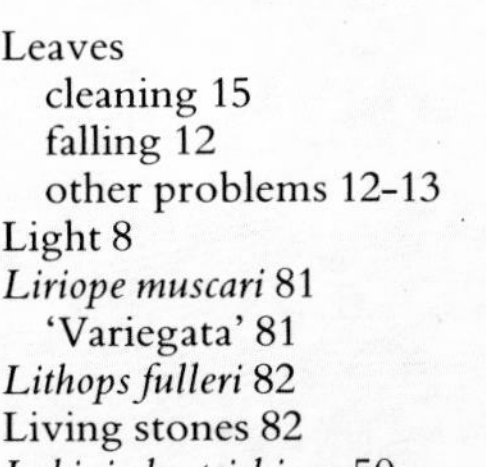

Picture Credits

The following pictures were supplied by Harry Smith Horticultural Photographic Collection.

a = above, b = below, r = right, l = left

pp 6, 34, 41, 44 al and ar, 50, 62a, 64, 65, 66, 70, 71, 77, 78b, 79, 81, 90, 91b, 94a, 95, 101a, 103a, 104a, 105al and ar, 108, 119, 120, 121.